'John hits the mark with this book: a practical and inspired approach that offers a structured framework to help anyone succeed.' **Martyn Proctor, Executive Director, Ernst & Young**

'I've read many books on organizational trust and John's is one of the best – a welcome addition and a must-read.' **Barbara Brooks Kimmel, CEO and Co-founder, Trust Across America**

'What this bold and thought-provoking book shows is that there is an urgent need to rebuild trust through developing leaders that don't just "talk the talk", but who also "walk the talk".' **Paul Kehoe, CEO, Birmingham Airport**

'Highly readable and addresses both the theory and the practice of the trust-building challenge.' **Jane Frost CBE, CEO, Market Research Society**

'The red-pill moment represents the choice between living the status quo or embracing a new reality. Well written, thought-provoking and practical – here's to the nice guys!' **Rob Edwards, Managing Director, FARM Digital**

'Written with an energetic and accessible style, John combines his personal experience with insight from research and executive interviews to outline a path for building truly trustworthy organizations.' **Steve Larke, Vice President, Capgemini**

'*The Trusted Executive* is a myriad of timeless wisdom, practical examples and great models demonstrated beautifully through a personal narrative.' **Kate Marshall, Vistage Board Chair and Executive Coach**

'A book that challenges the fundamentals of leadership and the role that leaders and organizations can play in society. Easy to read; it's a toolbox to help develop modern leaders.' **David Biggs, Managing Director, Network Rail Property**

'This is a thought-provoking, practical and inspiring book, which challenges staid approaches to leadership. A must-read that will change the thoughts and approaches of all who read it, such that they can make a positive and lasting difference in their own businesses.' **Larraine Boorman, CEO, Optima Group**

'Filled with personal examples, coaching sessions and CEO interviews, *The Trusted Executive* is a must-read for any existing or aspiring executive in any industry. Take the red pill now and develop the new habits of success.' **Lance McCarthy, CEO, Hinchingbrooke Health Care NHS Trust**

'*The Trusted Executive* is mindful, mind-bending and mind-expanding reading. I thoroughly enjoyed the balanced use of theory, research, personal examples and practical tools.' **Ingrid Riddervold Lorange, CEO, Global Shared Services, Telenor**

'In *The Trusted Executive*, John provides a provocative analysis of the skills that the forward-looking CEO needs to lead a firm through a world of disruptive and unsettling change.' **Andrew Parry, CEO, Hermes Sourcecap**

'*The Trusted Executive* will have significant value for leaders, and aspiring leaders, who need new perspectives and extra tools if they are to thrive in the coming years.' **Steve Thorn, Senior Vice President, CGI**

'*The Trusted Executive* is an invaluable, forward-thinking handbook for every existing or aspiring leader.' **Gina Lodge, CEO, Academy of Executive Coaching**

'An excellent resource for leaders seeking to improve their practice.' **Professor John Rudd, Warwick Business School**

'This is a well-researched and thought-provoking book. I would thoroughly recommend it to leaders in all sectors – it's time to take the red pill!' **Heath Monk, CEO, Future Leaders Trust**

'A compelling and inspirational book which presents a robust framework for a dramatically new style of leadership.' **Martin Mackay, Chairman and CEO, Experior Group**

'*The Trusted Executive* is a must-read for every executive who is serious about growing their business with a long term vision. Given recent headlines, this book has been launched at exactly the right time!' **Kannan Ramaswamy, Founder, Ganymede Advisory Partners**

'With *The Trusted Executive*, John Blakey has delivered an accelerated course to give today's leaders the knowledge, methods and tools to thrive in a 21st-century context.' **Frank Contrepois, Senior Director of Automation and Innovation, Virtustream**

'Brutally honest, John opens up his own life experiences, as well as a lifetime of research, to deliver a clear set of principles defining modern business. Trust him and you will fly. I'm glad I don't take the blue pill.' **Richard Hyams, Director, AStudio**

'If you want to succeed as a leader, you must become a trusted executive. John shows you how in this clearly written and highly practical gem of a book.' **Bob Vanourek, Former CEO of five companies and award-winning author**

'A highly enjoyable read.' **Martin Newman, CEO, Practicology**

'With *The Trusted Executive*, John knocks it out of the park! Amazing insights that can be easily applied whether you are a corporate leader, captain of a team, a mum or a dad.' **Rick Schaltegger, General Counsel, Microdynamics Group**

'This book is a must-read for all business leaders who believe that trust is inherently right, strategic and necessary for success.' **James Rouse, Vistage Board Chair and former CEO, Arrhythmia Research Technology, Inc.**

'*The Trusted Executive* provides a fascinating glimpse into the pitfalls to avoid and the proactive steps required to achieve your goals.' **Andrew Baud, Founder, Tala PR**

'John has set all CEOs a challenge! The examples given, the interviews presented and the insights provided made me think more deeply about trust as a fragile and critical key performance indicator. John, thank you for a great book!' **Alan Saunders, CEO, Illustra**

'*The Trusted Executive* should be a mandatory read for all those who sit in the boardroom of power.' **Jonathan Worsley, Founder and Chairman, Bench Events**

'*The Trusted Executive* offers practical guidance and actions to help leaders get to where they need to be.' **Jason Smith, CEO, Crestawood**

'The management book I've been waiting for! I am excited about applying what I have learnt in our own business.' **Robert Postlethwaite, Managing Director, Postlethwaite Solicitors**

'A refreshing, thought-provoking and inspiring book that will appeal to all courageous leaders. John challenges us to think differently to many traditional leadership norms.' **Kate Fletcher, Vistage Board Chair and Managing Director, XI-erate**

'I read this book in a single sitting. John's writing style drew me in and his practical examples are profoundly credible.' **Ben Meehan, CEO, QDATRAINING**

'You only get one reputation. In *The Trusted Executive* John brilliantly guides and inspires us to build that reputation.' **Andrew Orrock, CEO, Arkessa**

'John has done a masterful job of describing the nine leadership habits of trustworthiness. I was touched by his inclusion of kindness, humility and bravery.' **Kathy Green, Managing Partner, Executive Coaching Connections**

'We live in a time when businesses have an urgent responsibility to earn people's trust. In *The Trusted Executive*, John expertly identifies the skills that every leaders needs if they are to step up to this challenge.' **Guy Grainger, UK CEO, JLL**

'A powerful combination of well-researched theory and personal insight from first-hand experience. As a former colleague of John, I recognize his character authentically shining through this book.' **Seamus Keating, Chairman, First Derivatives plc and Mi-Pay Group plc**

The Trusted Executive

*Nine leadership habits that inspire results,
relationships and reputation*

SECOND EDITION

John Blakey

KoganPage

Publisher's note

Every possible effort has been made to ensure that the information contained in this book is accurate at the time of going to press, and the publishers and authors cannot accept responsibility for any errors or omissions, however caused. No responsibility for loss or damage occasioned to any person acting, or refraining from action, as a result of the material in this publication can be accepted by the editor, the publisher or the author.

Second edition published in Great Britain and the United States in 2021 by Kogan Page Limited

2nd Floor, 45 Gee Street
London
EC1V 3RS
United Kingdom
www.koganpage.com

122 W 27th St, 10th Floor
New York, NY 10001
USA

4737/23 Ansari Road
Daryaganj
New Delhi 110002
India

Kogan Page books are printed on paper from sustainable forests.

ISBNs
Hardback   978 1 78966 647 2
Paperback   978 1 78966 645 8
Ebook   978 1 78966 646 5

British Library Cataloguing-in-Publication Data
A CIP record for this book is available from the British Library.

Library of Congress Cataloging-in-Publication Data
Names: Blakey, John, author.
Title: The trusted executive: nine leadership habits that inspire results, relationships and reputation / John Blakey.
Description: Second Edition. | New York: Kogan Page Ltd, 2020. | Revised edition of the author's The trusted executive, 2016. | Includes bibliographical references and index.
Identifiers: LCCN 2020031493 (print) | LCCN 2020031494 (ebook) | ISBN 9781789666472 (hardcover) | ISBN 9781789666458 (paperback) | ISBN 9781789666465 (ebook)
Subjects: LCSH: Leadership. | Trust.
Classification: LCC HD57.7 .B5545 2020 (print) | LCC HD57.7 (ebook) | DDC 658.4/092–dc23
LC record available at https://lccn.loc.gov/2020031493
LC ebook record available at https://lccn.loc.gov/2020031494

Typeset by Hong Kong FIVE Workshop
Print production managed by Jellyfish
Printed and bound by CPI Group (UK) Ltd, Croydon CR0 4YY

'It is required of stewards that they be found trustworthy.'
Paul of Tarsus

CONTENTS

Conclusion: 'Well done, Blakey' 187

FOREWORD

I define courage as 'the ability to put the interests of others ahead of your own and be able to absorb personal risks'. Courage comes in many forms. There is the courage to lead a business. The courage to launch a new product or service. The courage to speak up for what you believe in. The courage to write a book. Frequently, courage involves anticipating the future; being prepared to act as if the future were happening today. This is what I hope we did at Unilever under my stewardship and this is what I sense John is doing in writing this timely book.

Yet, however courageous we are, it is also wise to seek help and guidance as we tread our path. I am grateful to all those who have helped me build my own career. I still seek that help today, whether it be through reading books, talking to trusted advisers or listening to business stakeholders. I know that this book will become a great source of help to many, many leaders. It is a manual for those executive leaders who are bravely anticipating the future and yet recognize they need input, inspiration, motivation, coaching and knowledge. It is a gold mine of tips, tools, insightful anecdotes and business best practice. It is a resource to keep close by your side.

For we know that we cannot change the business ecosystem on our own. Unilever is a powerful, global business, yet our ambitious 'sustainable living' goals could not be achieved without collaboration with governments, NGOs, pressure groups and partner organizations throughout the world. Similarly, we are not going to rebuild trust in business without a collective redefinition of the purpose of business and a thorough examination of the behaviours through which this purpose is achieved. It is through the research, writing and speaking of authors such as John that this rallying call is being issued to business leaders far and wide. It is then down to each one of us as to whether we are ready to heed that call.

I have little doubt that trust, not authority, is the only glue that will hold organizations together in a diverse, global, technology empowered world. But, as John points out, I fear that we have yet to grasp the scale of this trust-building challenge. It is not simply an issue of ability or an issue of integrity or an issue of benevolence; it is an issue of all three of these attributes being pursued day in and day out as an integral part of our executive leadership roles. Only through such a sustained and integrated approach will we combat the rampant scepticism that can threaten to take hold amongst customers, staff and the public at large.

Some of the medicine John prescribes through his nine leadership habits will not taste familiar or pleasant. We are well versed in the need to deliver results, to be honest, to be consistent and to coach others, but what are we to make of it when he urges us to evangelize, to be kind, to be humble, to show vulnerability and to be morally brave? Doesn't this fly in the face of the heroic leadership models in which we have traditionally placed great faith? Yes, it does and some will challenge the more idealistic edges of this work. Nevertheless, it would be a brave leader who gambled against this agenda becoming more dominant in the coming years.

In the balance between looking after today and preparing for tomorrow, we will continue to face difficult choices; John does not shirk from pinpointing exactly where these choices lie. As you read the book, it is difficult to resist the wall of evidence he has constructed from his own personal experience as a business leader, his rigorous academic research and the views of the many CEOs he has coached and interviewed. This comprehensive snapshot of the latest academic and practitioner thinking should give us all real pause for thought.

Thankfully, after issuing such a grand trust-building challenge, John readily acknowledges that we will all make mistakes as we grapple with these issues. It is reassuring to find a chapter that helps us recover quickly when things go wrong. As the CEO of a global company, I was conscious each day that trust is fragile; one rash word, one mistake, one accident can wreck many years of good work. It is difficult to recover trust but it is not impossible, and John provides wise counsel on this point.

As we pursued our 'sustainable living' vision in Unilever, we recognized the importance of individual leaders role-modelling specific behaviours. Setting this personal example is an important prerequisite in delivering change, but sooner or later it must be accompanied by other organizational shifts if the behaviours are to become hard-wired into the organization. Processes, metrics, structure, incentives and strategy are amongst the many factors that must fall into alignment with the new agenda. In this way, we create organizations that can be trusted out of leaders who can be trusted and these organizations then influence society as a whole. Unfortunately, this is a never-ending process because, as we change, the world changes and we must keep rewriting our own rules.

Overall, I am greatly encouraged that business leaders are stepping up to fulfil their potential as agents of trust and societal change. The unique value of books such as this one is that, through giving us a glimpse of tomorrow today, they accelerate the pace with which we create the future. They accelerate the progression and development of tomorrow's trusted executive. That is an exciting prospect and I congratulate John on adding his inspiring voice to the growing clamour for change.

Paul Polman
Former CEO, Unilever

Introduction

'You're too nice, Blakey'

Welcome to the journey

Managers manage. Leaders anticipate. This is a book about anticipation. A book about looking forward to a future where trustworthiness defines leadership. A book about ability, integrity and benevolence. A book about developing Nine Habits of Trust that are fit for a transparent world in which nothing can be hidden. The premise of this book is that the world is ready for a different breed of executive; a leader with transformational trust-building skills. If you want to anticipate and take the lead, if you want to be a pioneer in the 21st-century boardroom and deliver outstanding results, inspiring relationships, and build a cast-iron reputation for trustworthiness then this is a book for you.

But before we look forward, let us first look back. Some time ago, I was working with the sales leadership team of HP Americas in Dallas. Despite the intense schedule, I was determined to sneak away one evening and visit the JFK memorial museum. John F Kennedy, US president 1961–63, has always inspired me and it seemed appropriate to go and pay my respects. Nearby to the JFK museum there is a simple white 'X' painted on the road marking the exact spot where JFK was assassinated on 22 November 1963. As I stood and looked at that white cross, I pondered on why this man still had such a hold on the public imagination over 50 years after his death. After all, he was not a perfect leader, but it seems that people trusted him. Not everyone held this view, but large swathes of the western world did trust JFK and still do. What was it about this leader that built such trust?

JFK clearly had ability but then every US president has a measure of ability. JFK also had integrity; he spoke his truth and he appeared to be a man who knew right from wrong – not every US president can claim this characteristic! Yet most interesting of all, JFK appeared to be a benevolent man, a kind man, a man who took care of those less fortunate than himself. How many of his fellow presidents could claim a reputation such as this? It is this trio of qualities – ability, integrity and benevolence – that marked JFK out as a unique leader; a man of great trustworthiness. In many ways, he was ahead of his time. Far, far ahead. So far ahead that some would say that he paid for his vision with his life. JFK was a leader for tomorrow living in the '60s world of The Beatles, the rise of communism and the civil rights movement. However, we leaders of today live in a very different world; the world of Trump, Brexit, Climate Change, #MeToo, COVID-19 and fake news. A world where not only do we have more scope to build the three pillars of leadership trustworthiness, but we also sense the urgency surrounding this challenge. Today, trustworthiness represents both an opportunity and an imperative. PricewaterhouseCoopers (PwC) stated it well when they said:

> PwC's view is that the time has come for a new settlement between business and society – one based on less regulation and more responsibility... Businesses must seek to identify, develop and embed the right culture and behavioural norms that will earn both public trust and business success. This is the journey ahead.[1]

The purpose of this book is to help you navigate the journey ahead. This is a practical guide built on solid theoretical foundations. A guide informed by my own experience as a corporate leader, entrepreneur and executive coach, whilst also underpinned by my doctoral research at Aston Business School, interviewing over 70 CEOs and surveying over 500 board-level leaders. My aim is to bridge the world of academia and the world of business and provide you with a rigorous manual for inspiring trust using the Nine Habits of Trust. In so doing my hope is that you, the trusted executive of tomorrow, are inspired to learn, to practise and to pioneer.

Tomorrow's trusted executive

You might be an existing CEO or managing director who recognizes that the context of business is changing and wishes to keep ahead of the curve.

You might be an executive leader who leads hundreds or thousands of people around the globe and recognizes that leading a diverse, international team requires superlative influencing skills. You might be an aspiring high-potential executive in the 'marzipan layer' of corporate life, sandwiched between the baby-boomers of the boardroom and the 'Gen Y' agitators of your virtual office. You might be an entrepreneur grappling with the head-spinning implications of new technological trends. And finally, you might be someone like me: a coach, academic, consultant or colleague that is charged with helping these executive leaders be the best that they can be.

If you are in one of these categories, then you are important. Not because you have an impressive job title, a big salary or fast-track access through airport security, but because you influence the behaviour of people around you. As one academic guru concluded, 'If we want to understand why organizations do the things they do, or why they perform the way they do, we must consider the biases and dispositions of their most powerful actors – their top executives.'[2] Executive leaders are the 'bell-weather' individuals in their organizations. The findings of my own research demonstrate that the biggest single factor in building a high-trust organizational culture is the behaviour of the CEO and their senior leadership team.[3] In the words of one of the CEOs I interviewed, 'The only way you get trustworthiness into an organization's blood is if the top leaders have it in their blood.'

Do you have trustworthiness in your blood? Do you have the DNA of a trusted executive? Or do you have the DNA of the leaders that I first encountered in 1985 as a graduate trainee in utility giant British Gas? In the business environment of those days, the white western male ruled the roost with an iron rod; emotional intelligence was a dim and distant dream. What we now call bullying was an accepted rite of passage and none of us had really grasped the full implications of the Sirius micro-computer that sat in the corner of the office winking at us in black and green; we didn't yet grasp that technology would beget transparency and that transparency would undermine the traditional foundations of trust.

As a recently appointed young manager, I remember leaving the local office one day in my Citroën 2CV only to be chased down the drive by one of the admin clerks. She caught up with me and knocked on my window. I opened it and she breathlessly gasped, 'We've just been having a discussion in the office and we don't know what to call you?' 'How do you mean?' I replied. 'Well, do we call you John, Mr Blakey, Sir or boss?' I was fresh out of university and had just returned from a weekend away at a hippy music festival. The idea of anybody calling me 'Mr Blakey, boss or Sir' was bizarre. Yet this is how the world of business was just one generation ago; you were not on first-name terms with your boss. You were a distant Sir, boss or Mr Blakey. My guess is that tomorrow's trusted executive will face many more such culture-defining moments in the coming years. The questions will not be 'What do we call you?' but more likely, 'What is your position on climate change? How do you justify your salary? Is our supply chain protected from modern slavery? How come only 25 per cent of our board is female? What about the ethics of artificial intelligence?' How they respond to the innocent, and not-so-innocent, questions that will be asked by staff, customers, investors and the media will determine the profile of the modern business leader. In particular, their responses will either build trust with 21st-century stakeholders or destroy it.

Trust has to be your highest value

'Trust has to be the highest value in your company, and if it's not, something bad is going to happen to you.' These were the words used by Marc Benioff, CEO of Salesforce, at the World Economic Forum in Davos.[4] In a technology sector that had been hit by recent scandals and was subject to intense scrutiny, Benioff concluded that the most important item on the CEO's ticklist was not revenue, profit, customer satisfaction, product quality, supply chain efficiencies, talent development, digital marketing or international expansion but... trust! Echoing his sentiments, Jack Welch, ex-CEO of General Electric, says, 'Leadership today is all about two words: It's all about truth and trust.'[5]

Yet Marc Benioff and Jack Welch are not alone; many academic commentators have been predicting such a situation for many years. Back in 1975, the researchers Golembiewski and McConkie claimed that, 'There is no single variable which so thoroughly influences interpersonal and group behaviour as does trust.'[6] In 2002, Tony Simons and Judi Parks at Cornell University followed up by conducting a survey of more than 6,500 employees at 76 US and Canadian Holiday Inn hotels. They discovered that a one-eighth improvement in a hotel's score on leadership trustworthiness led to a 2.5 per cent increase in profitability. They concluded by stating: 'No other single aspect of manager behaviour that we measured had as large an impact on profits.'[7] My own research revealed that over 89 per cent of board leaders consider trust critical to attracting and retaining top talent, 91 per cent consider it critical to maintaining customer loyalty, and 88 per cent consider it critical to achieving sustainable bottom-line performance.[8] Meanwhile, Dr Paul Zak's research in 2016 found that, compared to employees of low-trust organizations, high-trust cultures report 74 per cent less stress, 50 per cent higher productivity and 76 per cent increased employee engagement. These statistics confirm Covey's claim that 'trust is the one thing that changes everything'.[9] Trust is a magic wand.

Yet if trust is so important, why do we understand it so poorly, measure it so haphazardly and destroy it with impunity? I have yet to come across a business that defined trust and tracked the key performance indicators directly associated with it. It is left to the professional bodies and academics to carry out this task. Their results do not always make for happy reading:

'The Future of Britain' report commissioned by media group OMD revealed that only 7, 6 and 5 per cent of the 2,000 Britons surveyed trusted banks, utility companies and insurance firms respectively.[10]

The 2017 Edelman Trust Barometer found that trust in business had fallen to record lows, with only 52 per cent of those surveyed trusting business 'to do the right thing' and only 37 per cent considering company CEOs to be credible spokespeople – a figure that had fallen 12 percentage points since 2016.[11]

A 2017 Gallup survey in the United States revealed that confidence in major institutions (including banks, media and government) had fallen to historic lows, with only 35 per cent of Americans stating that they could trust institutional leaders to do the right thing most of the time.[12]

Meanwhile, since the global financial crisis of 2008, a catalogue of business scandals have been featured in the media, including the 2010 BP Deepwater Horizon scandal, the 2012 rigging of the LIBOR inter-bank lending rate by Barclays bank, the 2015 revelation that VW had fitted over 11,000 emissions-cheating devices to its cars around the world, and the 2018 dismissal of Carlos Ghosn, Chairman of Nissan, for alleged financial misconduct. This deepening loss of trust in big business has prompted much soul searching amongst leaders and academics alike, prompting one author to conclude that 'our faith in many institutions has been dragged to a critical tipping point'.[13]

Against this alarming backdrop, if it is true that trust is the highest value in a company, then leaders will need to master this topic in the same way they mastered total quality management in the '80s, the learning organization in the '90s and social media marketing in the '00s. They will find ways to define trust, measure it and build it with persistence and passion. At first glance, trust may seem a slippery concept but, with effort and focus, it can be pinned down. It has its rules and its patterns, its short-cuts and its pitfalls. Trustworthiness is a skill that can be developed by both individual leaders and collective organizations. It is the purpose of this book to guide you through the trust-building maze and deliver you safely out the other side armed with a pragmatic and powerful trust-building toolkit.

The journey ahead

This is a book in three parts. In Part I (Chapters 1–2), we will explore how trust in executive leadership has been lost so that we can understand the scale and depth of the problem. We will review the traditional measures of success in business and therefore the traditional role of the leader: using intellect and authority to drive the single bottom line of profit. I will propose that this is a broken model and that what has broken it can be captured in one word: transparency. I will argue the case for an alternative model where the successful executives of tomorrow will use the three pillars of trust (ability, integrity and benevolence) to deliver a new measure of success – the triple bottom line.[14] The triple bottom line encompasses outstanding financial results, inspiring personal relationships and a cast-iron reputation in society as a whole. It is a sustainable model of business success befitting the 21st century. It requires the role of the executive leader to be re-cast from untrustworthy agent to trusted steward.

In Part II (Chapters 3–6), we will drill down into the detail of how to master trust-building leadership habits. The book will shift from exploring the theory of trust to studying its practice. As an executive coach, I have often been met with the frustrated cry, 'I know trust is important, John, but how do I 'do' trust'? Whilst I could offer my clients subjective opinions from my own and others' leadership experience, I could not offer them a rigorously tested scientific model of trust-building behaviours. It was this gap in the trust theory that became the focus of my six-year research into the behavioural habits of high-trust leaders and high-trust brands. As a result of this work, I created a unique Nine Habits of Trust model which identifies the nine habits and maps these to the three pillars of ability, integrity and benevolence to create the model shown in Figure 0.1.

FIGURE 0.1   The Nine Habits of Trust

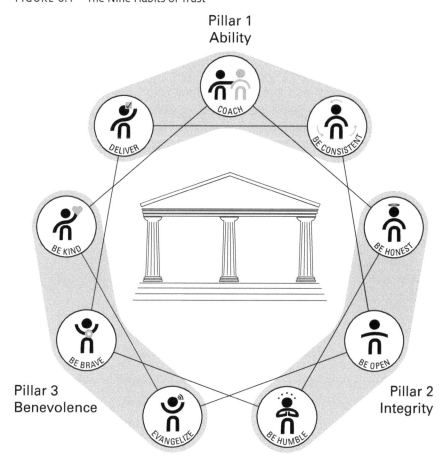

Armed with the Nine Habits of Trust, we can confidently build high-trust leaders and high-trust cultures that we know will lead to sustainable business success. For each of these nine trust-building habits we will look at practical models, tools and inspiring examples that will transform your leadership skills and your business brand. Through a unique set of questionnaires, we will assess your current level of trust against the Nine Habits of Trust model so that you can identify strengths and weaknesses and develop targeted action plans. We will also look at how the Nine Habits of Trust can be used to recover when mistakes are made; proven coaching techniques for bouncing back when trust is violated.

In Part III of the book (Chapter 7) we will learn from CEOs across different sectors who have worked with the Nine Habits of Trust model and used it to drive results, relationships and reputation through a variety of leadership development initiatives. The experience collated in Chapter 7 is from the work of the Trusted Executive Foundation – a not-for-profit consultancy I have founded to help leaders and their teams create a new standard of leadership defined by trustworthiness. The Foundation team have delivered keynotes, workshops and executive coaching programmes to leaders and their teams around the world and have also developed a variety of tools and resources to support these leaders in putting the theory of trust into practice. These tools include an online Nine Habits leadership survey that allows trust to be measured and benchmarked, together with an individual 360 feedback tool that allows leaders and their teams to receive detailed, objective feedback on their own trust habits. By sharing the experience of these leaders, the outputs from these tools and the learnings from these programmes, I hope this helps you map the theory of trust to the operational realities and pressures of front-line leadership

Throughout this journey we will embed the learning using a variety of tools and resources:

- case studies, relevant academic research and personal examples;
- insights into relevant coaching tools and techniques;
- excerpts from interviews with practising CEOs, non-executive directors and chairs;
- practical exercises to use with yourself and your teams;
- coaching conversations based on my experience of working with CEOs and their teams.

As with all good journeys, we aim to arrive promptly at a worthwhile destination, while also travelling in comfort and ease. We want to go fast enough to maintain a sense of progress, but not so fast that we miss something important. At the end of Chapters 3–5 I have created example CEO coaching conversations that focus on developing one or more of the nine leadership habits in more detail. These coaching conversations are waypoints on the journey. I would encourage you to use them as an opportunity to pause and consolidate the learning before pressing on with more new material.

There are many routes from A to B. I hope the route I have chosen to navigate in this book is both efficient and engaging. In particular, I hope the book appeals to both your head and your heart; enough logic, structure and rigour to stand up to critical analysis and enough passion, imagination and flair to keep you turning the pages at speed.

Igniting the spark

Finally, before we set off, let me explain briefly why I came to write this book. Writing a book and undertaking a doctorate are not challenges you take on lightly. Both are demanding, lonely tasks with long-term and indeterminate outcomes. Why does anybody commit themselves to such ventures? What sustains the long haul of reading, writing and researching? For me, there has to be a fire in the belly, an irrational passion, a cause to care about. How are such passions ignited? We are all unique individuals with our own defining experiences. Sometimes, in the midst of one of those defining experiences, a spark lights a fire within us. At the time, maybe we did not know the fire had been lit, but slowly it starts to consume us and draw us into its grip. It starts to demand its full realization.

For me, the spark ignited one day as I strolled through the corporate HQ as a recently appointed executive. The managing director of the company was walking towards me and said casually, 'How's it going, Blakey?' 'Great,' I replied. 'Yesterday, we closed the biggest deal we have ever done.' 'You think that's good, do you?' was the curt put-down. 'Yes, I think it's great,' was my defiant stand. At this point, a jabbing forefinger confronted me and I heard the damming words, 'You know your problem, Blakey – you're too f-ing nice!' And with that, the managing director in question marched off into the distance, leaving me stunned and bemused. My biggest problem was that I was too nice? What did this mean? Too nice to get to the top without cooking the books? Too nice to lead my team without bullying or harassing them along the way? Too nice to deliver outstanding results in the vaguely psychopathic world of corporate life?

I was grappling with these questions when deep down something visceral kicked in. A spark ignited; a fire had been lit. My determination was sealed. From that point onwards, I committed myself to demonstrate that 'nice folk', folk who can be trusted, can also deliver superb results and claim their place in the boardrooms of tomorrow. First, I wanted to demonstrate it through my own business career and then I wanted to demonstrate it through helping others who are pioneering on the same path. That fire drove me to help build a technology consultancy that was sold for £74.5 million in 1999, to then become a FTSE100 international managing director at the age of 37 and an award-winning entrepreneur at the age of 43. It drove me to become an executive coach, helping over 120 CEOs across 22 countries to achieve their goals, and writing the best-selling book *Challenging Coaching* with fellow nice guy Ian Day.[15]

The fire burned so strong that it drove me to then complete a doctorate on trust, to write this book, and to found the Trusted Executive Foundation. Along the way, I have met many 'nice folk' who are courageously pioneering in boardrooms around the world. These 'nice folk' inspire me daily with their determination, their resilience and their success. Despite my obvious ambition and drive, I aspire every day to be 'too f-ing nice' and I hope you do too!

Through this mixture of first-hand business experience and deep personal reflection, my own conclusion is that the 21st-century business world desperately needs the nice folk, for without them trust evaporates like a puddle on a hot summer's day. It needs leaders who know how to build trust using their ability, their integrity and their benevolence. To paraphrase Charles Green's writing in *Forbes* magazine, I believe the world needs leaders who rely upon the power of trust, rather than trust in power. The world needs leaders who are willing to re-wire their behavioural habits to meet the needs of a new generation of business stakeholders, leaders who are ready to renew their licence to lead in a socially inclusive, technology-empowered and radically transparent world.[16] If your instinct is to agree with me then this book will build that instinct into a firm conviction, it will inspire you with a compelling vision for the future, and it will equip you with the practical tools and techniques to deliver on that vision, day in and day out, amidst the hurly-burly of business life. It will ignite a spark. If your instinct is not to agree with me then you're welcome to come along too!

Endnotes

1 PricewaterhouseCoopers (2010) *Trust: The overlooked asset*, PricewaterhouseCoopers, London

2 Hambrick, D C (2007) Upper echelons theory: An update, *Academy of Management Review*, **32** (2), pp 334–43

3 Blakey, J S (2019) *CEO/Senior Leader Trustworthy Behaviours and their Role in Promoting Organisational Trustworthiness*, Aston Business School

4   Benioff, M (2018) Trust has to be the highest value in your company, *Salesforce*, https://www.salesforce.com/company/news-press/ stories/2018/012318/ (archived at https://perma.cc/PRE6-EAAT)

5   Roth, D (2015) Jack Welch says only two words matter for leaders today: truth and trust, *LinkedIn*, https://www.linkedin.com/pulse/truth-trust-crap- how-jack-welch-looks-leadership-today-daniel-roth/ (archived at https://perma.cc/ 8SS6-BLKZ)

6   Golembiewski, R T and McConkie, M (1975) The centrality of interpersonal trust in group processes, *Theories of Group Processes*, **131**, p 185

7   Simons, T (2002) The high cost of lost trust, *Harvard Business Review*, **80** (9), pp 18–19

8   Blakey, J S (2019) *CEO/Senior Leader Trustworthy Behaviours and their Role in Promoting Organisational Trustworthiness*, Aston Business School

9   Zak, P J (2017) The neuroscience of trust, *Harvard Business Review*, **95** (1), pp 84–90

10 O'Mahony, J (2013) Google 'as trusted as the Church' by Britons, *Daily Telegraph*, 30 April

11 Edelman, R (2017) 2017 Edelman trust barometer: Global report.

12 Brenan, M (2017) Americans' trust in government to handle problems at new low, *Gallup*, https://news.gallup.com/poll/246371/americans-trust-government- handle-problems-new-low.aspx (archived at https://perma.cc/7AAK-NHZD)

13 Botsman, R (2018) *Who Can You Trust?* Penguin, p 5

14 Jeurissen, R (2000) Cannibals with forks: The triple bottom line of 21st century business, *Journal of Business Ethics*, **23** (2), pp 229–31

15 Blakey, J S and Day, I (2012) *Challenging Coaching*, Nicholas Brealey Publishing

16 Green, C (2012) Why trust is the new core of leadership, *Forbes*, http://www.forbes.com/sites/trustedadvisor/2012/04/03/why-trust-is-the-new- core-of-leadership/ (archived at https://perma.cc/L3D8-RCTP)

PART ONE

Trust lost and trust regained

01

A broken model

The blue pill vs the red pill

> There is one and only one social responsibility of business – to use its resources and engage in activities designed to increase its profits so long as it stays within the rules of the game, which is to say, engages in open and free competition without deception or fraud.[1]

Such was the opinion of the economist Milton Friedman when interviewed for the *New York Times* back in September 1970.[1] This quote is a great example of how truth is defined by the times and the culture in which we happen to live. Truth is not a fixed entity. I am sure that if I was a US businessman reading Milton Friedman's article back in the 1970s it would seem an entirely reasonable conclusion being spoken by a highly eminent economist. Yet it is now history. The world has changed and it keeps changing.

Friedman's quote reveals that we have lived in a business world that worshipped the concept of financial profit. This singular pursuit was fuelled by executive leaders who relied upon one central assumption: if I have a powerful enough intellect to work out the best answers and I have the authority to implement those answers then I will maximize the financial returns of this business. I will be successful in the eyes of the business owners. We worshipped profit and the temple of financial profit was supported by two sacred pillars – intellectual ability and authority (see Figure 1.1). I am not using the word 'authority' in the context of being an expert on a topic or even as the enforcer of agreed standards, policies and rules. I am using it in the context of a job title in a hierarchical organization, which grants an executive leader the authority to tell someone else what to do.

FIGURE 1.1   The temple of profit

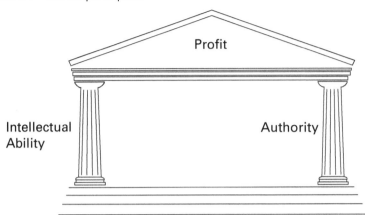

This model had the benefit of being both simple and, for many years, largely effective in achieving the goal. We could regard it as a product of the industrial revolution – a highly mechanistic, scalable means of production. However, can you imagine if I had teleported a 1970s businessman into a 21st-century boardroom and placed him amongst his modern-day peers? What would he have made of their smart phones and their video conferencing, their tie-less, smoke-free conversations on the rise of Generation Y, their strange habit of pouring their own coffees at the break? Not to mention that the lady sat at the table is not a minute-taking secretary but the CEO herself! That businessman would be as bewildered as I hope you were when you read the above quote from Milton Friedman.

In this chapter, I will explore the background to this model: who created it, why they created it and the purpose it has served. In particular, I will examine the underlying assumptions that this model makes about the trustworthiness of executive leaders and conclude that it is a model that remains deeply wired in the executive subconscious. While this model has served the world of business to a point, I will argue that it is reaching the limit of its effectiveness in a 21st-century environment where the converging trends of globalization, technology, media, Generation Y and diversity are exposing that authority has been used as a surrogate for trust. In other words, what held the traditional model together and enabled it to function was deference to authority. When this pillar is challenged by the diverse stakeholders of the modern business, the model starts to break down. Authority is what we use when we want to manage staff for the singular pursuit of financial profit on behalf of the owners of the business. Trust is what we must use if we want to lead a diverse group of stakeholders who all wish to have a say in the future purpose of business and who all wish to benefit from its activities. So let us explore more closely how and why the '70s world of Milton Friedman differs from the world of tomorrow's trusted executive.

Traditional measures of business success: Single bottom line

Traditionally, life was simple. The purpose of a commercial business was to maximize profits and this was the singular measure of success. Even in 'third sector' organizations such as charities and social enterprises, we have been trained to focus upon another version of profit, which we call 'surplus'. Whatever we call it, profit has given us a barometer of success that has some advantages and some disadvantages. On the one hand, it is a readily under-stood concept in the business world and it is a consistent measure of the added financial value of our activities. On the other hand, it breeds a myopic fascination with one particular assessment of business contribution that can blind business leaders to the wider context in which they operate. If business continues to worship profit within a societal context that has decided it no longer worships profit then this will progressively undermine trust in busi-ness institutions and those who lead them.

Where does this idea of worshipping profit come from? It comes from Friedman's 19th-century peers such as Adam Smith and other economists who ushered in the industrial revolution. It is 19th-century economics that still lies at the heart of the modern business system. Smith and his protago-nists created a model of man in which 'economic values guide choice, and choices are rational and utility maximizing... the goal of Smith's economic man is to maximize the wealth of the firm and is based on contractual duties owed to owners'.[2] This is a model of man in which the source of power is institutional authority and intellectual ability. The means of managing risk is through control, not through high-trust relationships. This is a model of man in which we are all no more than 'self-interested actors rationally maxi-mizing our own personal economic gain'.[3] This mindset powered a period of unprecedented growth and innovation in the western world, yet we must be careful to remember that it was only ever a model; it was not the truth. Like all models, it has its limitations. Despite those increasing limitations, it is highly likely that this model remains the underlying assumption of your organizational world; an assumption so deeply wired into our collective consciousness that we have long forgotten its origin and its justification.

However, we have not forgotten its central implication: as executive leaders, our job is to maximize profit for the owners of the enterprise. How could we forget this implication when these same owners monitor, control and reward us daily with this goal in mind? If you are an entrepreneur that owner may be the voice of your venture capital investors. If you are a charity then it is the voice of your trustees. If you are a global CEO it is the quarterly return you present to your shareholders. Whatever your form of governance, I guess that you will quickly identify this voice and recognize its impact on your leadership behaviours. As one of the global CEOs I interviewed put it:

> However much you try to avoid it, the quarterly reporting matters and that drives a set of behaviours that are at odds with longer-term goals. You talk about driving the business for the long term but you act to deliver in the short term. Consequently, it appears as if you are lying.

The goal matters. What matters gets measured. And what gets measured gets done and so creates a deep groove in the organizational psyche.

CASE STUDY

The case of Dodge brothers versus Ford Motor Company

The ideology of short-term shareholder profit as the sole purpose of business was enshrined in law via the legal dispute between the Dodge brothers and Ford Motor Company.[4] In 1919, Henry Ford, the founder of Ford Motor Company, sought to end special dividends for shareholders to make long-term investments in new plant and machinery, which would also increase the number of people employed by the company and reduce the cost of Ford cars to the consumer. Announcing his intention, he said:

> My ambition is to employ still more men, to spread the benefits of this industrial system to the greatest possible number, to help them build up their lives and their homes. To do this we are putting the greatest share of our profits back in the business.

The Dodge brothers, John and Horace, owned 10 per cent of the company at the time and, on behalf of the minority shareholders, they challenged Henry Ford's decision in a court of law. The case of the minority shareholders was that they did not see that it was appropriate for Henry Ford to run the company as a 'charity'. The court upheld the view of the minority shareholders, demanding that the company pay an extra dividend of $19.3 million. Announcing his decision, the judge stated:

> A business corporation is organized and carried on primarily for the profit of the stockholders. The powers of the directors are to be employed for that end. The discretion of directors is to be exercised in the choice of means to attain that end, and does not extend to a change in the end itself, to the reduction of profits, or to the non-distribution of profits among stockholders in order to devote them to other purposes.

The case established a precedent that the balance of power between shareholders and other stakeholders, such as the executive leaders, employees and customers. A great deal has changed in the business culture since 1919; it is unlikely that a CEO of today would be accused of running a charity if he or she announced plans to re-invest profits in the long-term future of the business. However, the case study does remind us of the history and depth of single bottom line thinking in the business and legal system.

The traditional role of the executive leader: Untrustworthy agent

This focus on profit has defined the role of the executive leader since the industrial revolution because, at its heart, this model rests on the assumption that the executive leader cannot be trusted. Economists refer to this mindset as agency theory.[5] In agency theory there are two key roles: the owner of the organization and the agent who implements the owner's will. These days we refer to those 'agents' as the leaders or managers of the organization, but the word 'agent' still captures their original economic function. According to agency theory, if you leave 'agents' or executive leaders to their own devices they will seek to exploit the situation for their own benefit because they are motivated purely by their own rational self-interest. Hence the executive leaders must be monitored, controlled and incentivized heavily to align their interests with those of the owners of the business. Agency theory built a business world that didn't need trust and it made sense if the sole purpose of business was to maximize profit for the owners. In that world, the role of the executive leader is to be an untrustworthy agent.

In his fascinating paper 'Bad management theories are destroying good management practice', Professor Sumantra Ghoshal explores the full implications of this statement, concluding that:

> Many of the worst excesses of recent management practices have their roots in a set of ideas that have emerged from business school academics over the last 30 years. In courses on corporate governance grounded in agency theory we have taught our students that managers cannot be trusted to do their jobs.[6]

More worrying, he then proceeds to argue that these theories have a habit of becoming self-fulfilling: 'A theory that draws prescriptions on corporate governance on the assumption that managers cannot be trusted can make managers less trustworthy.' In other words, if you are an executive leader subject to a labyrinth of control systems then there is no need to develop trustworthiness because, in theory, there is no risk left to manage. If you still insist on behaving in a trustworthy manner then your ability, integrity and benevolence will be attributed to the presence of the control systems rather than to your own leadership character. In the agency theory world, you are damned if you do and damned if you don't; you are an untrustworthy agent because the system needs you to be that way.

One of my colleagues, Dr William Tate, summed it up for me when we were sat in a meeting at the Chartered Management Institute discussing the implications of the global financial crisis of 2007–08 on leadership development. A series of experts were asked their opinion and various worthy suggestions were put forward. The microphone was passed to Dr Tate, who calmly said, 'It's not about the fish'. While everyone's head was spinning with the introduction of this blunt metaphor, Dr Tate went on to explain:

> We keep taking the fish out of the fish tank, putting them on special diets and building them up to be super-fish and then we put them back in the same toxic water they came from. It's not about the fish. It's about the fish tank. It's not about the leaders. It's about the leadership culture of business. It doesn't matter how well you develop the leader; if you simply put them back into the same toxic leadership culture you took them out from you will get the same toxic leadership behaviours.[7]

It's not about the fish. It's about the fish tank. An organizational 'fish tank' built on agency theory will always tend to produce untrustworthy agents as its leaders. And those leaders will build an organizational culture based on the same underlying principles; organizations that become populated by layers of untrustworthy agents, all of whom need to be monitored, controlled and incentivized.

In my own career, it took me 13 years to work out that this underlying agency theory world was driving my own leadership behaviour and the behaviour of those around me. In a flash, as I listened to Dr Tate, it explained to me why, when I walked into the office as an executive leader, I was no longer expected to be a human being. It explained to me why it always felt like I was being pushed to be this 'nasty-boss-person' who didn't trust anybody else. It explained to me why my intellect was prized so highly and my heart and spirit were being systematically dismantled. A model that is based on distrust needs no heart and no spirit; it just needs clever folk who can manipulate others to serve the singular goal of profit. In this model, my role as untrustworthy agent was to demonstrate to you how clever I was and to control you via my authority because you, like me, cannot be trusted. We were all untrustworthy agents together!

Now I understood why, as an untrustworthy agent, I had to be separated from the people I led; if I wasn't separated from them by my dress code, my office, my higher manager's canteen, by the company car I drove and by the language I spoke, then the illusion that they were fundamentally different from me might start to break down. The dangerous possibility that I might find them trustworthy might creep into the equation. This notion had to be resisted at all costs, because if I started to discover an underlying level of human trustworthiness then the whole agency theory model would start to be questioned.

As an analogy, think of the scene in the cult classic film *The Matrix* where our hero, Neo, is offered a choice between taking the blue pill or the red pill. The blue pill will keep Neo in the computer-generated reality of the matrix, while the red pill will reveal to Neo the painful truth of the illusory world and 'unplug' him from the matrix. Neo's leadership mentor, Morpheus, gives him the following advice:

> This is your last chance... You take the blue pill – the story ends, you wake up in your bed and believe whatever you want to believe. You take the red pill – you stay in Wonderland, and I show you how deep the rabbit hole goes.

In the film, Neo takes the red pill and confronts the shocking truth: the world he had lived in was simply a clever illusion. Had he taken the blue pill he would have stayed in the illusory world; comfortable, yet blind to the sinister reality that governed his life. The red pill/blue pill choice is a parable about seeking the greater truth in a situation and challenging your existing belief systems. Taking the red pill is a frightening step to take because, in the moment you get a step closer to the truth, you will also have to step out of your comfort zone to engage and adapt to a new perception of reality. In these terms, I realize now that for the first 13 years of my career as an executive leader I was taking the blue pill as prescribed to me by agency theory economists. And all those around me were taking the blue pill as well. We didn't even think there was a choice. It was a blue pill world, a blue pill fish tank, and that was the way it worked. You told people what to do and, if they didn't do it, you told them again, because you knew more and they knew less. You had the authority and you had a bigger brain and that's all you needed in the blue pill world. But then it started to change...

The red pill: Transparency

Over the past 20 years the traditional paradigm of business leadership has been buffeted relentlessly by five converging trends: globalization, technology, media, Generation Y and diversity. In isolation, each of these trends is powerful. Taken together, they become revolutionary. Taken together, they become the game-changing red pill of executive leadership. It is not my intention to describe each trends in detail as many other texts already do an excellent job of this. However, it *is* my intention to examine further the common thread that runs through each of these trends: transparency. Transparency is the red pill; the pill that opens your eyes to the fact that the traditional agency theory model of business is broken. As one CEO I interviewed put it, 'You've got to be open, honest and transparent with the good, the bad and the ugly. There is no such thing now as "you don't know" or "you don't understand". Those excuses are things of the past.'

The truth is that pre-internet we were living in an extremely well-contained world. A privileged, masculine, western world in which information was limited in its scope and its access. In the absence of pervasive technology and media, the availability of information was relatively easy to control. In the absence of a long-term global perspective, the economic exploitation of one country by another was considered 'fair game'. In the absence of Generation Y, Generation X and the baby-boomers were still subservient to authority; readily trusting in a fashion that now seems naive. In the absence of non-white males in the boardroom, leadership discussions were inevitably narrow and self-serving. In sum, even untrustworthy agents with good intentions were making decisions based on a fraction of the available data. Untrustworthy agents with less benign intentions were deciding which fraction of data suited their own purpose and maximizing their own economic returns. This was all made possible by a lack of transparency.

Even in the early 2000s, large corporations were still persisting with this traditional leadership paradigm. At this time, I was international managing director in a global IT organization. White Western men populated our boardrooms. The CEO did not have a PC on his desk. If we had trouble in foreign subsidiaries, we would send the latest home-grown hot shot to 'sort things out'. The command and control culture was alive and kicking. Profit was king and we danced to the City's tune. We would routinely manage the flow of information both internally and externally to suit the shareholder agenda. For example, as we approached the financial year-end, those working in the company always felt the company was about to go bust because there were such dire cost-cutting measures and fresh announcements about a new round of redundancies. Once the financial year concluded, we would pick up the papers to read that our company had reported another record year and paid a generous dividend. The cycle repeated itself with mind-numbing predictability year after year and it worked... for a time.

Contrast this with the situation 20 years later. There is a relentless drive to create more diverse boardrooms in terms of gender, age and ethnicity. Often we focus upon the moral dimension of this trend, yet it is equally significant from a perspective of transparency. A diverse boardroom has access to a broader range of opinions, perspectives and data. Customers, suppliers, investors, activists, alumni and staff are sharing information via the internet and social media.

The case of David Dao highlighted the game-changing impact of transparency. Mr Dao was a Vietnamese-American passenger 'escorted' from the overbooked United Airlines flight 3411 as it prepared to fly from Chicago O'Hare International airport on 9 April, 2017.[8] After the incident, the immediate reaction of the CEO of United Airlines, Oscar Munoz, was to claim that Mr Dao was removed from the flight for being 'disruptive and belligerent'. In the blue pill, agency theory world that would have been the end of it. We would have believed the CEO and got on with the rest of our lives. Unfortunately, in this transparent, red pill world, the story then took a revealing twist. It turned out that, at the time Mr Dao was being 'disruptive and belligerent', several passengers were videoing the incident on their iPhones. What we later saw, beamed around the world via social media, were two burly security guards dragging Mr Dao down the aisle of the plane with blood pouring from his mouth. In the background, we heard passengers shouting 'No!', 'Stop!', 'Oh my God!'. In the next 48 hours, over 480 million people in China watched the video clip – United Airlines' biggest market. The company's share price fell 4 per cent, wiping £1bn off its market value. At this point, Oscar Munoz, the CEO, had a 'road to Damascus' moment and decided that 'this incident should never have happened and we will be reviewing our policies and procedures accordingly'. Of course, by that point, it was too late because trust in business had already taken another blow. As a researcher on trust, transparency is the gift that won't stop giving. Every week I have a new case study from somewhere around the world where a blue pill leader attempts to play by the old rules of agency theory and is exposed by the red pill of transparency.

Meanwhile, the topic of climate change has alerted us all to the stark reality that we operate in one global system that has its own limits, patterns and long-term challenges Millennials are flocking into the workplace, prompting commentators such as Bob Moritz, US Chair of PricewaterhouseCoopers (PwC) to comment:

> When I was coming up, we knew what we were doing, but we didn't ask why we did it... [Back then] I would have been astonished that PwC's Millennials don't only demand to know the organization's purpose... but are [also] prepared to leave the firm if that purpose doesn't align with their own values.[9]

These younger generations demand transparency because it is at the core of the technology-enabled world in which they have grown up. They don't worship profit and they don't expect the organizations they work for to do so either.

According to Ben Page, CEO of market research company Ipsos MORI, 'Our surveys show that only 29 per cent of the public believe that the people in charge know best and this percentage is dropping with each successive generation.' In the past, in the absence of knowledge, we erred on the side of trusting those in authority. Nowadays, in the absence of knowledge, we assume that something is being deliberately hidden. This is a fundamental shift because it reveals that it was only deference to authority that was holding the old model together. If we had authority then people trusted us because really they had no choice. Yet mistakenly we then started to confuse authority with trust and think that they were the same thing. Those in authority grew lazy in their trust-building skills, because enough people were still giving them the benefit of the doubt. The Ipsos MORI statistics show this strategy will no longer work. There is no 'benefit of the doubt' left; there is just a yawning scepticism. Using authority as a surrogate for trust is now a 'busted flush'. Drawing on an example from the world of politics, one CEO I interviewed captured this neatly when he said:

> So if we think of politicians fiddling their expenses. The sums involved might not be huge and there might be reasons why it happened but the real issue is that the public say, 'Well, if they fiddle their expenses then what else are they fiddling?'

So now we are all being offered the red pill of transparency. Technology, diversity and media have made it more readily available, globalization has made it more necessary, and the younger generations have claimed it as their staple diet. It is transparency that is exposing a broken agency theory model. As Warren Buffett quipped, 'Only when the tide goes out do you discover who's been swimming naked'.[10] There's been a lot of skinny-dipping in the world of executive leadership. We got away with it in the blue pill world because we could hide stuff and because people still believed us. Now people have seen what we have been hiding and, as a consequence, they do not believe us anymore. This is the transparency double-whammy that stalks today's corridors of power. Academic researcher Fiammetta Borgia caught the spirit of the times when she said:

> [The] endless gathering, manipulating [and] retrieving of information has created the new transparency imperative. The public's right to know is steadily and inexorably eroding the secret, opaque lives of corporations... the more we know the more we demand to know [and] the more there seems to disclose. The cycle seems endless.[11]

It was Don Tapscott and David Ticoll who first heralded the revolutionary impact of the age of transparency in their prophetic book *The Naked Corporation*.[12] I thoroughly recommend that book to readers who want to delve further into this topic. But it is time for us to move on. Let us now examine the impact of transparency on the executive leadership role.

Impacts of transparency

Transparency allows us to see things that we couldn't see before. It is like the moment that you suddenly 'click' when staring at an optical illusion. For those who have not seen the illusion in Figure 1.2 before, at first glance you may believe you are seeing a picture of a young woman looking over her right shoulder. However, if you stare for longer and imagine the chin of the young woman could also be the hooked nose of a much older lady, then your perception will flip and you will see a different picture. That is what I call a red pill moment. Where once you saw only a beautiful young woman, now you see a haggard old lady. And once you have seen what was originally hidden, you can never look at the image in the same way again. Similarly, when I look at executive leadership through the lens of transparency I can now see two different images. Back in the '70s, I only saw Friedman's beautiful young woman maximizing profit to fuel the industrial revolution. Now, I still see that beautiful young woman, but I also see the haggard old lady. I can no longer ignore the ugly side of business. What is more, I don't think I am alone. More and more of your stakeholders are seeing the haggard old lady of the 'agency theory' business:

FIGURE 1.2   Old lady or young woman?

- They will see her whenever you use your authority to hide information from those who need to know it.
- They will see her whenever you fail to show empathy and compassion for those who are impacted by your actions in the wider world.

- They will see her whenever you use your intellect divorced from your heart and your spirit.

- They will see her whenever you maximize economic returns for yourself or for your company by exploiting the wellbeing of others.

- They will see her whenever you are insensitive to the needs and concerns of those who are different from you, whether that difference be measured by gender, ethnicity or age.

And what we see of business becomes its reputation and its brand.

CASE STUDY

Facebook and Cambridge Analytica

Facebook was everyone's darling. Not a nasty bank, or a dirty oil company, but a bastion of the technology-enabled democracy. A Silicon Valley success story whose mission was to 'give people the power to build community and bring the world closer together'. We dared to trust that its CEO, Mark Zuckerberg, was a purpose-driven, wide-eyed geek, not another cynical, blue pill agent looking to extort and fleece. We had put a lot of trust in the new dawn of internet-driven technology, which is what made it all the more disappointing when, in 2018, we read how 80 million Facebook profiles had been harvested by the 'This Is Your Digital Life' app and then the data illicitly made available to Cambridge Analytica.[13] With Orwellian guile, Cambridge Analytica had subsequently used this data to implement micro-targeting of political advertising to swing marginal voters in various political elections.

Like many CEOs before him, Mark Zuckerberg initially missed the point. In true 'blue pill' style, he and his team sought to argue that there had been no actual data breach and therefore that Facebook had done nothing wrong. Facebook's General Counsel rightly stated, 'The claim that this is a data breach is completely false. People knowingly provided their information, no systems were infiltrated, and no passwords or sensitive pieces of information were stolen or hacked.' Technically this was correct, but the real scandal of the story was not that Facebook did anything illegal but that the 'red pill' of media scrutiny had revealed the real mission of the organization. It suddenly appeared that Facebook's mission was not to 'give people the power to build community and to bring the world closer together' but rather to 'amass personal data, extract that data and use it to allow other parties to exploit and manipulate people indiscriminately'. With 98 per cent of Facebook's revenue coming from targeted advertising, how could its business model be anything else? What angered us about the Facebook scandal was the feeling of being let down by the very people you thought had come to save you.

The Cambridge Analytica incident plunged Facebook into the biggest reputational crisis of its 14-year history. Mark Zuckerberg was hauled in front of the United States Congress and had his own 'road to Damascus' moment when he stated that the company did not do enough to prevent Facebook being used for harm, including 'fake news, foreign interference in elections and hate speech'. During the testimony, Zuckerberg apologized for the breach of trust, saying, 'It was my mistake, and I'm sorry. I started Facebook, I run it, and I'm responsible for what happens here'. Ultimately, the company was fined $5 billion by the Federal Trade Commission for 'privacy violations'.

At its heart, the Cambridge Analytica scandal is not a story about Facebook but a story about how digitally fuelled transparency is revealing the reality of the agency theory model. Increasing numbers of people are weighing up whether they want to remain as passive 'blue pill' economic consumers, or whether they wish to speak out as 'red pill' citizens rebelling against the prevailing institutional dogma. Ironically, Facebook, originally a digital disruptor of institutional trust, has now become one of the distrusted institutions. If Facebook can fall foul of such scrutiny then what are the risks for other organizations who remain wilfully blind to the gathering inquest?

Whether you are an executive leader in a global corporate or an entrepreneur in a young start-up business, the lessons of the United Airlines and Facebook cases are clear. Transparency has changed the world and it will *keep* changing the world. Be careful, because the issues that will be top of your agenda tomorrow may not even be on your radar today. Like Oscar Munoz and Mark Zuckerberg, part of you will be tempted to cry out, 'It's not fair. I'm only a businessman. It's not my job to save the world.' And you're right, it is not your job to save the world but it is your job to listen to your stakeholders and anticipate where their agenda is heading. Your stakeholders include your owners, but they also include your customers, staff, partners, suppliers, regulators, politicians, the media and the public at large. Those who fail to anticipate the diversity and breadth of the coming social agenda risk losing trust overnight. Losing trust means losing your brand reputation and losing your licence to lead.

Those who have most to lose from the age of transparency are those who gained most from opaqueness. For many, the red pill is going to be a bitter pill to swallow. Yet once we've swallowed it we can get on with the task of building a new model and rebuilding the trust that has been lost. Because if we're not going to worship profit any more, what *are* we going to worship? And if we can't rely upon our authority to get things done, what will be the superglue that holds us together in this new world? I hope you find these intriguing and exciting questions. However, if you choose to stick with the blue pill then good luck and don't delve any further into this book – it may corrupt your mind!

There is no purple pill

We have covered a lot of ground in this chapter and used the blue pill/red pill metaphor to explore what I have proposed is a broken business model. The chapter started with a picture representing the traditional model of business – a temple to profit supported by the pillars of intellectual ability and authority. Having explored how transparency is undermining traditional authority, we can update that picture to reflect the current reality; see Figure 1.3.

FIGURE 1.3   A broken model

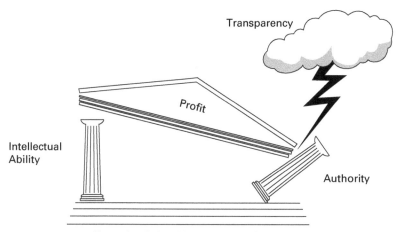

Executive Role – Untrustworthy Agent

Transparency is the lightning bolt that strikes at the pillar of authority. That pillar can only take so many blows before it crumbles and falls away leaving a dangerous 'Trump-shaped' leadership vacuum in our institutional lives. The pace at which this shift is occurring varies from sector to sector and from country to country. The leader's job is to assess the risk of relying upon this traditional 'blue pill' model versus waking up to the new 'red pill' reality. This needs careful judgement. Jump too quick and you are too far ahead of the wave. Jump too late and you've missed the moment.

Since the first edition of this book, I have delivered this message to thousands of leaders globally on behalf of the Trusted Executive Foundation. In these workshops, I challenge leaders to think carefully about the choices they make. At the break in one such conference, a participant approached me and said, 'You know what you need at this point in your workshop. You need two jelly beans – a blue one and a red one. You need to put them in the palm of your hands and stand in front of the audience, Morpheus-style, saying 'I'm offering you a choice. A choice between the blue pill world that trusts in power and the red pill world that relies upon the power of trust.' I followed the suggestion and it went down well. I now add the following extra clarifications:

> I can't force you to take the red pill. It's an invitational model. But this is
> a choice you are making every day when you walk into the office. It is an
> ideological stance. You are either taking the blue one or the red one. There is no
> purple pill. You can't be half-pregnant.

It's time to decide where we stand. It is time to make new choices. Amidst the ruins of a broken model, business requires a new architectural design: a design that will build trust with all the diverse stakeholders of the 21st-century business. The nature and construction of that design is the focus of our next chapter.

POINTS TO PONDER

- What is the counter-argument that suggests that, even in today's age, the role of business is solely to maximize profit?

- How often are you still relying on the authority of your job title to get things done? When is this appropriate and when is it a surrogate for a lack of trust?

- You may think I have been overly harsh on the blue pill world of agency theory. What are the positive aspects of this model that may still serve us in the red pill world?

- What are the examples in your business that reveal the 'haggard old lady' of traditional business? How can you challenge and change these practices?

- What is the specific impact of the red pill of transparency on your business? What actions does your business need to take to stay ahead of the transparency curve?

- What is the most recent example of red pill embarrassment that has occurred in your business sector?

Endnotes

1 Friedman, M (2007) *The Social Responsibility of Business is to Increase its Profits*, Springer, New York

2 Key, S (1999) Toward a new theory of the firm: A critique of stakeholder 'theory', *Management Decision*, 37 (4), pp 317–28

3 Davis, J H, Schoorman, F D and Donaldson, L (1997) Toward a stewardship theory of management, *Academy of Management Review*, 22 (1), pp 20–47

4 Henderson, M T (2007) *Everything old is new again: Lessons from Dodge v. Ford Motor Company*, University of Chicago Law & Economics, Olin Working Paper (373)

5 Jensen, M C and Meckling, W H (1976) Theory of the firm: Managerial behaviour, agency costs and ownership structure, *Journal of Financial Economics*, 3 (4), pp 305–60

6 Ghoshal, S (2005) Bad management theories are destroying good management practices, *Academy of Management Learning & Education*, 4 (1), pp 75–91

7 Tate, W (2013) *Managing leadership from a systemic perspective*, Centre for Progressive Leadership, White Paper, January

8 Crowther, K (2017) *United Airlines Public Relations Crisis*, Report

9 Moritz, B (2014) How I did it... The US Chairman of PwC on keeping millennials engaged, *Harvard Business Review*, 92 (11), pp 41–44

10 Friedman, T L (2009) Swimming without a suit, *New York Times*, 21 April

11 Borgia, F (2005) *Corporate Governance and Transparency Role of Disclosure: How to prevent new financial scandals and crimes?* American University Crime and Corruption Center, Washington, DC

12 Tapscott, D and Ticoll, D (2003) *The Naked Corporation: How the age of transparency will revolutionize business*, Simon and Schuster, New York

13 Cadwalladr, C and Graham-Harrison, E (2018) Revealed: 50 million Facebook profiles harvested for Cambridge Analytica in major data breach, *Guardian*, 17 March, p 22

0 2

The three pillars that inspire trust

In this chapter we will contrast the broken model of Chapter 1 with a new vision for building trust, which rests on three pillars. We will see that the three pillars that inspire trust involve reframing the role of the executive leader from untrustworthy agent to trusted steward. We will examine more closely the difference between trust and trustworthiness and so create a new model that clarifies how executive leaders inspire trust through focusing on their ability, their integrity and their benevolence. But first let us reconsider the purpose of business. If business does not exist solely to maximize profit for the owners, what is its purpose in a modern world?

Reflecting on the meaning of business back in 1954, Peter Drucker famously said, 'Profit is like oxygen. You need it to survive, but if you think that oxygen is the purpose of your life then you're missing something.'[1] Drucker's comments hinted that profit was simply the passport into a bigger game of business but his prophetic message was largely ignored for 50 years. It is only more recently that attention has focused upon the purpose of business and whether it should be serving a bigger role on the 21st-century stage.

On Tuesday, 16 January 2018, the CEOs of some of the world's largest organizations received a letter from an influential investor, Larry Fink. Mr Fink is Founder and CEO of Black Rock, a firm that manages $6 trillion of investments and a bedrock capitalist institution. In the letter, Mr Fink issued an exciting challenge – 'Society is demanding that companies, both public and private, serve a social purpose. To prosper over time, every company must not only deliver financial performance, but also show how it makes a positive contribution to society.'[2] Fink contended that companies who fail to do this 'will ultimately lose their license to operate'. Effectively, Black Rock was putting CEOs on notice that if they wanted the firm's continued support they must demonstrate a positive contribution to society as well as generating profit.

Some might have thought this was an isolated 'flash in the pan' from a maverick institution, but it is a trend that is increasingly gathering pace. On 19 August 2019, the influential US-based Business Roundtable group (BRT) issued a statement whereby it changed the official definition of the purpose of a corporation from 'maximizing profits for shareholders' to 'improving our society by looking out for employees, caring for the environment and dealing ethically'.[3] The BRT is no left-wing, minority pressure group. It comprises the CEOs of 181 of the US's largest corporations including Amazon, Apple and JP Morgan. Like the Black Rock statement before it, the BRT shift of stance triggered a flurry of media coverage, with commentators speculating as to whether it was a tipping point, or whether these were fine words with limited substance.

Then a further heavyweight brand of the business world weighed into the fray. On 16 September 2019, the *Financial Times* launched its 'New Agenda' brand platform under the strapline 'Capitalism – Time for a Reset'. Commenting on the launch, *FT* editor, Lionel Barber, said:

> The liberal capitalist model has delivered peace, prosperity and technological progress for the past 50 years, dramatically reducing poverty and raising living standards throughout the world. But, in the decade since the global financial crisis, the model has come under strain, particularly the focus on maximizing profits and shareholder value. These principles of good business are necessary but not sufficient. It's time for a reset.[4]

Finally, on 4 December 2019, the US PR firm, Edelman, published the results of a survey of 610 institutional investors in the UK, US, Canada, Germany, Japan and the Netherlands.[5] For the first time, Edelman was able to provide a snapshot of the investor perspective on trust, and the results made for fascinating reading:

- 84 per cent of investors agreed that maximizing shareholder returns can no longer be the primary goal of business and that business leaders should commit to balancing the needs of shareholders with customers, employees, suppliers and local communities.

- 86 per cent agreed that their firm would accept a lower financial rate of return to invest in a company that addresses sustainable or impact investing considerations.

- Over 50 per cent believed that ESG (environment, social and governance) practices such as healthy company culture, a diverse executive team and addressing societal issues had a positive impact on trust.

- Over 70 per cent believed having a high-trust reputation is important for attracting and retaining the best employees, winning new customers, growing market share and increasing market valuation.

- Investors regard the CEO as the most important steward of trust, followed by the CFO and board of directors

In light of these rapidly changing expectations regarding the purpose of business, we can expect a significant shift away from the agency theory model in the coming years. Companies will need to measure success in a broader, more holistic fashion than has previously been the case. In the new model of business, we will need to shift from measuring success via the single bottom line of profit to measuring success via the triple bottom line of results, relationships and reputation.

The future measures of business success: Triple bottom line

The 'triple bottom line' is a term that was first popularized by John Elkington.[6] The phrase took off in the period 1999–2001 and is now incorporated into many reporting standards around the world. It is often referred to as 'profit, people and planet' but I refer to it as 'results, relationships and reputation' since I think this constitutes a more grounded, practical definition. Until now, however, the triple bottom line has been consigned to the role of an accounting standard rather than a broader credo of leadership. For many executive leaders it is still a new concept and one that is not fully incorporated into daily business life.

The triple bottom line sits in contrast to the single bottom line discussed in Chapter 1. Financial performance remains a critical component of success, but it is the minimum entry level into the game. Alongside the pursuit of profit, the second bottom line is the people, or relationships, performance of an executive leader. Examples of leadership goals in this area could be:

- We will become listed as one of the top 100 employers by the Great Place to Work Institute.

- We will achieve staff survey satisfaction scores averaging 8.2 out of 10.

- We will reduce our staff turnover from 17 to 12 per cent in the next 12 months.

The third bottom line represents a new level of aspiration beyond both financial results and people relationships. Here, tomorrow's executives spread the net further to set goals that influence their reputation in wider society. 'Ah, so you mean corporate social responsibility (CSR)' I hear you say. Well, yes and no. Yes, the third bottom line aligns with CSR goals because we are talking about the social reputation of the firm. But no, this is not the same as CSR because it is not a corporate responsibility that is outsourced to a specialist role ('Head of CSR'). In the blue pill world, CSR was a bolt-on to the traditional model. In the red pill world, the triple bottom line represents an entirely different 'modus operandi'. It is not a bolt-on, it is a fundamental redesign of the operating philosophy of a modern business. You could look at it as a transition from corporate social responsibility to individual social responsibility. In the same way that having a human resources (HR) function does not remove the people responsibilities of individual executives, having a CSR specialist does not remove the individual societal responsibilities of every leader in the business. Examples of goals for the third leg of the triple bottom line would be:

- We will raise £5 million for a local charity and involve over 20 per cent of our staff in this project over the next three years.
- We will launch and sponsor a global industry award for the most eco-friendly business in our sector.
- As CEO of the company, I will make a stand on issues such as racism, social justice and climate change and use my voice to actively influence these social agendas.
- As a global pharmaceutical company, we will eradicate malaria from the world within five years.

The triple bottom line requires goals that are focused on relationships and reputation as well as financial results. Having read the above goals for the second and third bottom line, I would like you to compare the impact of those goals on your own motivation and energy compared to these single bottom line goals:

- We will increase the share price of our company by 20 per cent over the next five years.

- We will reduce our inventory costs by $1 million in the next 12 months.
- We will become a Fortune 100 company by 2020.
- As CEO, I will trigger my long-term incentive plan through hitting my financial targets.

I hope you can sense the shift from an agency theory world of economics and reason to a new post-industrial world where the world of business is re-humanized via a focus on socially meaningful outcomes. We are not machines. Financial goals tick boxes in our heads, but they are not the sort of goals that get us to spring out of bed on a cold, wet winter's morning shouting, 'Let me at it!' Financial goals are losing their impact because they are yesterday's story of business and no one can get too excited about living in the past. Tomorrow's trusted executives will focus on a new story that sets goals for the triple bottom line of results, relationships and reputation. These broader goals will motivate and engage not just Millennial talent inside the organization but also socially aware citizens who are looking to be more discerning about how they spend their hard-earned disposable income.

CASE STUDY
Unilever – a case study in the triple bottom line

When it comes to 'big business', they don't come much bigger than Unilever. This global consumer products company has 155,000 employees, annual revenues of more than $50 billion and sells its products in 190 countries. When former CEO, Paul Polman, was appointed in 2009, his first act was to stop the quarterly financial forecasting of Unilever's results to the City. Later, in an interview, he was asked why he did this on day one of his new role. He replied 'I figured I couldn't be fired on my first day'.[7] That was a measure of Paul Polman's courage in changing the traditional 'blue pill' mind-set at Unilever.

Under Polman's leadership, Unilever launched the 'Sustainable Living Plan', a bold triple bottom line vision which aimed to halve Unilever's carbon footprint and increase its social impact whilst also doubling sales and increasing long-term profitability. A 2018 review of the plan revealed the following progress:[8]

- Unilever's 'Sustainable Living' brands accounted for half of the company's growth and were growing at twice the rate of the rest of the business.
- 56 per cent of Unilever's agricultural raw materials were sustainably sourced, more than halfway to the 2020 target.

- Since 2008, CO_2 emissions from energy and water in manufacturing had reduced by 52 and 44 per cent respectively.

- Unilever had improved the health and well-being of 1.24 billion people around the globe through programmes on handwashing, safe drinking water, sanitation, oral health, self-esteem and skin healing.

When Polman stood down from his post in 2019, the Unilever share price stood at $42 – a rise of 350 per cent since the start of his tenure! Commenting on the sustainable living plan, Paul Polman said:

> We are at a turning point in history, a point where we all need to change for human life on the planet to continue to prosper. A new business model with sustainability at its heart is vital for quality of life around the globe to improve. Only the businesses that grasp this will survive. Only those who grow sustainably will thrive.[9]

The Trusted Executive Foundation helps leaders implement a triple bottom line strategy via our fellowship boards. Each board comprises 12–14 CEOs who are committed to building high-trust cultures in their organizations. The groups meet on a bi-monthly basis and, as part of the induction to the board, each member is challenged to set triple bottom line goals. These are reviewed with the group to ensure they are courageous, tangible and inspiring. Then, at each meeting, the members check in against their goals, highlighting what is working well and where they need help to improve. The process ensures peer-level accountability and drives a concerted focus on results, relationships and reputation. Shown below are examples of goals that members have set under each heading:

- Results:
  - Be the preferred supplier to two multinational organizations within the next 12 months.
  - Open our first office in New York within the next three years.
  - Achieve a £120m turnover at 5 per cent net margin by the end of the decade.

- Relationships:
    - Achieve a 10 per cent average improvement in employee engagement scores in our next annual staff survey.
    - Launch a national mental health initiative across our organization.
    - See my daughters and read to them before bed one night per week.
- Reputation:
    - Halve our carbon footprint in the next three years.
    - Organize a charity bike ride in South Africa for our employees and clients.
    - Become a national spokesperson for diversity and inclusion in the construction sector.

Trust and trustworthiness

FIGURE 2.1   The new business model

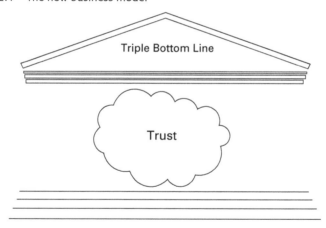

In building a new business model, Figure 2.1 shows that we have installed a new God in the temple of business – the triple bottom line. We noted from Chapter 1 that authority isn't a sticky enough glue to hold the model together anymore, so we need a new glue: the superglue of trust. Trust is a word we trip out daily yet how many of us know what it really means? How many of us understand what inspires trust? Thankfully, a host of academic researchers have been grappling with these questions while we have been busy running businesses. These researchers have worked hard to pin down the concept of trust and its close cousin, trustworthiness. Their rigorous and precise work enables us to build robust models of trust that stand the test of time. Let us briefly review their significant findings.

Despite a universal view as to its importance, there is little agreement as to the definition of trust.[10] Here is a sample of definitions that have been suggested over the years:

> [Trust is] a judgement of confident reliance on a person, organization or system, when there is an element of risk and uncertainty.[11]

> Trust consists of a willingness to increase your vulnerability to another person whose behaviour you cannot control, in a situation in which your potential benefit is much less than your potential loss if the other person abuses your vulnerability.[12]

> [Trust is] a psychological state that comprises the intention to accept vulnerability based upon positive expectations of the intentions or behaviour of another.[13]

You can see that the topic quickly gets complicated. Thankfully, all the definitions of trust agree on three common characteristics:

- trust involves taking a risk;
- trust involves keeping a positive expectation that the other party will not let you down; and
- trust has rational, emotional and moral components.

In other words, based on rational, emotional and moral computations I come to a conclusion that, on balance, I have positive expectations of your future behaviour and therefore I am going to take the risk of trusting you.

You, the executive leader, cannot control whether someone else will trust you but you do have one powerful tool that influences this outcome: your own trustworthiness. The only piece of the trust equation that you can control is your own behaviour and we describe this as your trustworthiness. The concept of trustworthiness can be defined as a state in which an individual or a firm 'is worthy of the trust of others'.[14] Trust and trustworthiness are often confused yet the vital distinction is that you can choose to be trustworthy but only others can decide whether they trust you.

In this new model, your goal is to become worthy of the trust of others. This distinction becomes increasingly important in a world where the red pill of transparency fuels a rampant scepticism. In such an environment, pursuing trust can feel like chasing your own shadow. In contrast, pursuing trustworthiness is like fixing your eyes on a distant lighthouse in the midst of a storm: it provides a reliable reference point. In the words of Solomon and Flores, 'In the ideal case, one trusts someone because she is trustworthy, and one's trustworthiness inspires trust.'[15]

The three pillars: Ability, integrity and benevolence

Our academic colleagues have also shone their forensic light on the word trustworthiness. They have had some fine debates as to the components of trustworthiness. In the 1970s, Professor John Gabarro of Harvard Business School suggested that trustworthiness resulted from the ability and character of the leader, with ability defined as the skills and knowledge to be successful in the required role and character comprising two further attributes of integrity and benevolence.[16] In the 1980s, other researchers countered by proposing a set of five characteristics of trustworthiness – integrity, competence, consistency, loyalty and openness.[17] Later, in the 1990s, Professor Aneil Mishra and his colleagues defined trustworthiness using the four dimensions of competence, openness, reliability and care.[18] Thankfully, in 2007, along came Shawn Burke and her research team at the University of Florida to summarize a 30-year debate and conclude that all models of trustworthiness consisted of three common pillars: ability, integrity and benevolence.[19]

Ability

The pillar of ability refers to our professional competence to fulfil the core task of executive leadership: delivering results. You can be as nice as you want to me and honest and open and caring, but if you keep letting me down in terms of delivery, your trustworthiness will be shot. I've worked with a lot of salespeople who I would have trusted implicitly to look after my own children, but I did not trust them to bring in the next big deal. I used to say to them, 'The problem is that I'm beginning to lose trust in you.'

It surprised them to hear the issue presented in that way. But it was the truth and, sooner or later, it ended up coming back to bite them. Time and time again, the issue of delivery came up in my interviews with CEOs. You can pick up from the following quotes that this is not an area where CEOs see much room for debate:

'Trustworthiness is delivering what you say you're going to do.'

'Trustworthiness is about doing what it says on the tin.'

'Number one: deliver on your promises. If you say you are going to do something then do it.'

Integrity

The second pillar of integrity refers to the extent to which we 'walk the talk'. We need to be reliable in our behaviours and consistently live up to the values and standards we have set for ourselves and the organization. Integrity has an ethical component: it implies honesty, openness and being fair. When I hear people assessing the promotion potential of their team members, the individual's integrity is often the first topic on the agenda. It is surprising how good people's memories are when it comes to recalling slips in integrity. A client of mine decided to block the promotion of a highly able leader based on a false expense claim that had been submitted many years ago when the individual had first joined the company. This minor transgression had permanently dented the perception of that individual's integrity. In my interviews, here is what CEOs said about integrity:

'You can test for integrity in an interview and see if the interviewee pushes back and says "No, I wouldn't do that, it is wrong." I want people who can stand up and say "no".'

'I would expect integrity in every employee.'

'The question about integrity is probably the most important one when it comes to checking references for a new employee – do you have any reason to question the integrity of this individual?'

Benevolence

The third pillar of benevolence refers to our concern for the well-being of others. The word comes from the Latin words *bene* and *volent*, translated as 'wishing well'. Benevolence is the opposite of malevolence. We show our good wishes to others through care, generosity and kindness. I have been in many a boardroom where the leader has publicly humiliated a member of the team through put-downs, sarcasm and withering personal criticism. Those leaders were highly able and as honest as the day is long, but they were not trusted. We could get away with that in the blue pill world because we used authority as a surrogate for trust. Increasingly, this approach will not work in a world where transparency dissolves the traditional levers of authority. While the CEOs I interviewed did not use the precise word 'benevolence', you can detect its presence in the following quotes:

'The most powerful destroyer of trust is when you feel the other person is acting in their own best interest and not yours.'

'A lack of care for the principal stakeholders destroys trustworthiness. Selective care to deliver short-term results. Cherry-picking so that you can live another day.'

'CEOs low on emotional intelligence will always struggle to generate trustworthiness.'

When I first came across the three pillars of trustworthiness, it was the third pillar of benevolence that intrigued me most. In 30 years of leadership development, I had yet to come across this word in any leadership competency framework. I had never been on the 'Introduction to Benevolence Course for Senior Leaders'. I had not been mentored in compassion, generosity or kindness. I pondered why this had been the case and then I realized that the agency theory model did not need benevolence to achieve its goal of profit. The agency model outsourced benevolence to other institutions in society. If you brought it into your leadership role then it was a 'nice to have' by-product of being a human being but not a 'must-have' attribute of leadership. If we require the new model of business to be built on trust then it is time to insource benevolence. It is time to re-humanize the workplace. I hope that is an exciting prospect!

Putting together the three pillars of trustworthiness gives us the following formula:

trustworthiness = ability × integrity × benevolence

Note that this is a formula involving multiplication, not addition. By the laws of maths, there are two unavoidable consequences of the trustworthiness formula:

1 if you score a zero on any one of ability, integrity or benevolence then your trustworthiness will also be zero;

2 if you score highly on all three pillars then your trustworthiness will grow exponentially since big numbers multiplied by big numbers produce even bigger numbers!

Executive leaders who focus on building ability, integrity and benevolence in parallel are practising trustworthy leadership. In focusing on the three pillars, we work equally hard to develop our ability to deliver results, our integrity to 'walk the talk' and our benevolence to do well to others. What is more, we set this example in our behaviour, not just with the owners of our business but with all the diverse stakeholders of the modern corporation – staff, customers, suppliers, media, government and the public at large. If we do this rigorously and consistently, we will build reputations as trustworthy leaders.

The future role of the executive leader: Trusted steward

FIGURE 2.2   The three pillars that inspire trust

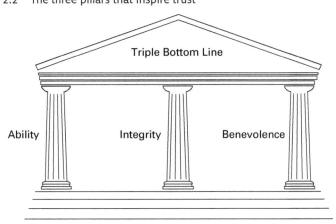

Executive Role – Trusted Steward

We can now update our new business model to include three new sacred pillars – ability, integrity and benevolence (Figure 2.2). These are the three pillars of trustworthiness that support the new purpose of the triple bottom line. Our new model is almost complete, but, finally, we must consider the role of the executive leader operating within this model.

A new measure of success, the triple bottom line, and the new glue of trust, create a vacancy for a different type of executive leader – a vacancy with a new job description. Tomorrow's executive leader will not be Chapter 1's untrustworthy agent driven by one dominant owner to produce a singular measure of success. In contrast, tomorrow's executive leader will balance the diverse and dynamic expectations of a web of stakeholders. She or he will be a steward. A steward is defined as 'one who rises above the level of an agent and is committed to the welfare of all stakeholders'.[20] In more practical terms, stewardship is 'the willingness to be accountable for the well-being of the larger organization by operating in service, rather than in control, of those around us'.[21] Stewards inspire trust by redefining the purpose of business to deliver triple bottom line goals and then putting themselves and the organization in service of those goals.

Stewardship theory sits in contrast to agency theory as an alternative model for business design. While agency theory has its roots in 19th-century economics, stewardship theory has its origins in 20th-century psychology. It rests upon a different model of people. If you recall, untrustworthy agents had to be controlled lest they exploit their leadership position for their own short-term personal gain. In contrast, stewardship theory assumes that the executive leader is responsible, socially aware and trustworthy. A leader that can be trusted – shock, horror! This risky starting point creates a different context for designing an organization. It creates a different 'fish tank'. For, as we learnt in the previous chapter, leadership theories tend to be self-fulfilling. A relationship that starts from an assumption of trust will tend to produce more trustworthy leaders. How does this happen? Let's take the example of control mechanisms. In an agency theory mindset, the leader must be controlled and monitored. Therefore, if I am controlled and monitored then naturally I am going to control and monitor my team likewise. In a stewardship mindset, the executive leader is given more discretion and freedom and you will tend to find that the executive leader's team are given more discretion and freedom likewise. Trust begets trust. As the late Professor Ellen Whitener of the University of Virginia put it: 'Managers' actions and behaviours provide the foundation for trust and it is... management's responsibility to take the first step and initiate trusting relationships'.[22] It starts with you.

TABLE 2.1   Comparison of agency theory and stewardship

Leadership Characteristic	Agency Theory	Stewardship Theory
Primary Goal	Economic	Self-actualizing
Driver of Behaviour	Self-serving	Collective-serving
Motivation	Extrinsic (ie for the love of the rewards of the job)	Intrinsic (ie for the love of the job)
Power Base	Institutional (job title, authority level, structure)	Personal (expertise, relationships, influencing skills)
Leadership Philosophy	Focused on control of others	Focused on involvement of others
Means of Managing Risk	Control mechanisms	High trust relationships
Organizational Ethos	Cost control	Performance enhancement
Timeframe Considered	Short term	Long term

As we contemplate the stewardship mindset, the blue pill versus red pill choice looms once again. To trust or to control, that is the question. If I start with trust I am a steward. If I start with control I am an agent. There is no in-between stance. To help you work out where you stand, look at Table 2.1, which contrasts these two positions in more detail.[23]

When I think of my own experience I realize that, despite their good intentions, the corporate organizations in which I worked were fundamentally agency-wired; their first instinct was to control via institutionalized authority. There was the odd exception and the occasional leader who created a stewardship bubble, using high-trust relationships to create exceptional results, but as soon as the bubble grew a greater force promptly burst it. I wasn't taught about agency theory on my MBA so I never understood the origins of this greater force and I didn't have the time to work it all out for myself. But I knew it didn't feel good. My personal survival strategy was to flee the mainstream organization and work on change projects. I found that amidst significant organizational change, such as the implementation of new IT systems, the prevailing agency mindset reached the limit of its effectiveness and a stewardship mindset was reluctantly tolerated. There was a freedom and relief that came from working with passionate, high-trust teams focused on long-term organizational improvement. The trick was to recognize that these teams were only a temporary blip. Those who thought that they heralded a new dawn of leadership enlightenment were often left feeling disillusioned and betrayed when the project came to an end and 'business as usual' was re-established. If you wanted to avoid being branded a maverick troublemaker then you needed to get onto the next 'brave new world' project as quickly as possible. For me, this strategy worked for a surprisingly long time, hopping from one change project to another like a frog jumping across water lilies; never staying long enough to sink and drown. However, after 20 years my time was up. I ran out of water lilies and the only leap left was to hop right out of corporate organizations and set up my own business.

Upon founding my own business, I discovered that I finally had the opportunity to carry out a full-scale experiment in stewardship. Some of the CEOs I interviewed shared a similar motivation. One made me smile when he said:

> I set up this company partly to create a different culture to the big banks where I had worked previously. We can run a business model where it's better to have a hole in the team rather than an asshole in the team. That's not possible in a plc environment.

In my first business, a coaching practice called 121partners, we did not start with a strong enough focus on the triple bottom line of results, relationships and reputation. The focus on measuring success only via financial performance still had too firm a grip on our thinking. I am now wise enough to see that we got that part wrong. I also underestimated the degree of agency conditioning in both myself and in others. Stewardship requires the leadership team to step up to a new level of responsibility, commitment and collaboration. We made significant steps in the right direction but, when the global financial crisis struck, our growth stalled. It was a fascinating experiment in stewardship but it was far from the finished product.

Learning from this, when I founded the Trusted Executive Foundation, I decided that from day one we needed a triple bottom line purpose. We chose a mission to create a new standard of leadership defined by trustworthiness and to donate all the profits from that work to UK-based Christian-led charities that are inclusive at the point of need. As a not-for-profit, we immediately created a different dynamic in terms of the talent we attracted, the customers we worked with and the measurement of our success. We also work hard as a leadership team to 'eat our own dog food' in terms of becoming trusted stewards and role-modelling ability, integrity and benevolence in our personal leadership. In so doing, we have experienced first-hand how much hard work is required to step up to this new benchmark. There are inevitable tensions between the three pillars of trust but at least we now have a language to discuss these tensions and so make better-informed decisions. As we learn ourselves, it equips us better to help others who will need to tread this challenging path.

These first-hand experiences have made me realize how difficult it is to implement the new business model and the stewardship mindset wholeheartedly. Yet I remain convinced that it is the 'fish tank' of the future. New and younger leaders will bring fresh insights and attitudes to help crack the puzzle. It is an incredibly exciting time to be a leader because there is a need for creativity, experimentation and learning.

Trust regained

Can you imagine what it would be like to work in a team or a firm where every individual is committed to maximizing their trustworthiness, where every leader is working on the three pillars, where every performance appraisal is focused on ability, integrity and benevolence? Can you imagine being a customer of such an organization or a supplier or a co-owner? How different would that experience be to the business environment in which you operate today? I hope this is an intriguing and exciting vision. Furthermore, I hope that you can see how this would be good for business, good for people and good for the wider world. I imagine you would take pride in being the steward of such an organization; to place it in your care and to give it your all.

This vision is exciting because it starts with each individual leader focusing on their own trustworthiness and it ends with more and more people choosing to give their trust. It ends with the creation of high-trust cultures in teams, firms and professional communities. And since business activity is so integral to our daily lives, a high trust business culture can be a major driver in creating a high-trust society. This doesn't happen overnight because there are many factors involved in choosing to trust and not all of them are in the leader's control. But it does happen one conversation at a time. As one CEO put it:

> You need to build trust over time; it doesn't happen instantly no matter how charismatic you are, how good you are. It takes time. But, like an onion that grows by adding layer upon layer, trust happens when trustworthy behaviours are reinforced, reinforced and reinforced.

We need to be patient and what justifies that patience is the long-term reward of high-trust cultures.

Back in 1995, Francis Fukuyama wrote the book *Trust: The social virtues and the creation of prosperity*.[24] It has sat on my bookcase for 20 years and it remains unread. It was a touch too heavy and academic for me, but I liked its underlying message. Fukuyama's premise was that economic life and social life are deeply interconnected. Furthermore, he ventured that only societies that foster high levels of trust will be able to sustain the large-scale business enterprises needed to compete in a global economy.

For Fukuyama, trust is a source of social capital that has a distinct value. So what is the size of the high-trust prize? In their 2018 report 'The Bottom Line on Trust', consultancy firm Accenture estimated that 54 per cent of the 7,000 US companies involved in its research had experienced a material drop in trust which they conservatively equated to losing out on revenues of $180 billion over a period of 2.5 years.[25] The report concluded:

> The numbers speak for themselves. Trust – as it relates to competitiveness – is so important to a company's bottom line that C-suite leaders downplay it at their own risk. The ability to manage and measure trust as part of your company's strategy has become a key competitive advantage.

So we have seen that through building trustworthiness at the individual level we can ultimately regain trust at the organizational and societal levels. We can claim the high trust prize, but it starts with you and I role-modelling the three pillars of trustworthiness. You may have heard of the story of the young boy walking on the beach after a storm. The storm had left thousands of starfish stranded on the beach and, every so often, the boy bent down, picked up a starfish and threw it back into the sea. An old man sat idly watching and was finally prompted to walk up to the boy and ask him what he was doing. 'I am saving the starfish,' the boy replied. 'You'll never save all these starfish. There are thousands of them on this beach, you won't make any difference,' countered the old man. At this, the boy bent down, picked up a starfish and threw it back in the sea. He turned to the old man and said 'Well, I made a difference to that one.' Similarly, we might conclude that regaining trust is too big a challenge for one executive leader to undertake. Our equivalent of throwing a starfish into the sea is to stretch our trustworthiness skills to new heights each working day. In this way, we become part of the solution rather than part of the problem. We are then leading by example.

In the CEO interviews I conducted, 'leading by example' was the most frequently cited responsibility of the executive leader in the challenge of building trust. Here is a selection of their comments:

'The trustworthiness of a business comes from the person leading the business.'

'If you're a corrupt CEO the organization will be corrupt.'

'If our politicians and business leaders are perceived to be untrustworthy then it is very difficult for others to think they should behave any differently.'

'You lead from the top – it's difficult to lead from the bottom.'

'It goes back to the leadership of the organization. If it is someone who is not straight or honest at the top then that is going to be reflected in the behaviours of the entire organization.'

As we draw this chapter to a close, it is time to present you with an alternative vision to the temple ruin that concluded Chapter 1. In that broken model the red pill of transparency acted as a bolt of lightning to shatter the traditional pillar of authority in a business world driven only to maximize profit. In that world the executive leader was cast as an untrustworthy agent. Our new vision is that the three pillar model is a tool for restoring trustworthiness in a business world pursuing the triple bottom line of results, relationships and reputation; a world where the executive leader is cast as a trusted steward (see Figure 2.3).

The three pillars of ability, integrity and benevolence correspond to the head, the spirit and the heart of leadership. Using different language we might term this IQ, SQ (spiritual intelligence) and EQ (emotional intelligence) of leadership. The trusted steward balances the development of these three aspects of resourcefulness to bring each to bear on the challenges of executive leadership. Note that the pillars are of equal height and so play an equal role in achieving the triple bottom line outcome. Trustworthy

FIGURE 2.3   The three pillars that inspire trust

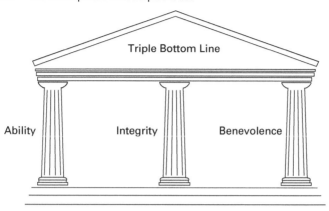

Triple Bottom Line

Ability   Integrity   Benevolence

Executive Role – Trusted Steward

leaders have the sensitivity to recognize which attribute is required in a given situation and can flex dynamically to bring ability, integrity or benevolence to the fore.

Typically, when we start our leadership career we have a bias to rely upon one pillar at the expense of the others. For me, as someone who followed a mathematical and scientific path in my education, it became natural in my 20s to lead with the head. The spirit and the heart were largely dormant in my executive behaviour. In my 30s, principally due to finding my religious faith, I brought the spiritual resource into play more actively and, as a result, worked hard on my integrity. Only when I became an executive coach in my early 40s did I realize that my heart skills, my benevolence, remained underdeveloped. Training and practising as an executive coach have been a revelation to me as regards the power of benevolence. For the first time in my career, I have been assessed against competencies that included the words 'care', 'empathy', 'sensitivity' and 'giving'. It has been a culture shock and one that has rightly shaken up my view of leadership. What I learn daily as a coach is to lead with my heart and to trust the transformational impact this has on the people with whom I work.

So where are you? Which is your dominant pillar and how has your leadership journey developed? What inspires your ability, your integrity and your benevolence? Where is your comfort zone and where is the edge of your learning? My own experience tells me that these attributes can be developed through practice, through feedback and through education. Some aspects will come more naturally to us and, in other areas, we will need to work harder. I was born left-handed but I know that, with practice, I could write perfectly well with my right hand too. The bigger question is whether I have the motivation to make the change. What is the payback for all the hard work? If one day I woke up and my left arm was paralyzed I'd quickly learn how to write with my right hand. If one day you wake up and find that your leadership is paralyzed then you will quickly develop the new skills you need to achieve your goals.

Managers manage. Leaders anticipate.

POINTS TO PONDER

- What are the triple bottom line goals for your organization? Are these goals cascaded through your organization so that every leader is evaluated against results, relationships and reputation?

- Think back over your career. Which organizations that you have worked for exhibited agency cultures and which were stewardship environments? Who is the leader you respect most as role-modelling stewardship behaviours? What specific behaviours do you see him or her demonstrate?

- What are the implications of recognizing that you can't control whether people trust you but you can control your own trustworthiness?

- Do you think there are more than three pillars that create trustworthiness in addition to ability, integrity and benevolence? Think of other qualities that demonstrate trustworthiness. Do they fit into this model or do they challenge its simplicity?

- I have painted a largely negative view of the traditional business mindset. What are the exceptions to the rule that challenge this standpoint? Where has the traditional business mindset made a positive contribution? What are the risks of focusing on trustworthiness at the expense of other leadership responsibilities?

Endnotes

1 Drucker, P (1954) *The Principles of Management*, New York

2 Sorkin, A R (2018) Black Rock's message: contribute to society, or risk losing our support, *New York Times*, https://www.nytimes.com/2018/01/15/business/dealbook/blackrock-laurence-fink-letter.html (archived at https://perma.cc/SCT7-M96E)

3 Business Roundtable (2019) Business roundtable redefines the purpose of a corporation to promote 'an economy that serves all Americans', https://www.businessroundtable.org/business-roundtable-redefines-the-purpose-of-a-corporation-to-promote-an-economy-that-serves-all-americans (archived at https://perma.cc/NKH4-3N7V)

4 Financial Times (2019) FT Sets the Agenda with New Brand Platform, https://aboutus.ft.com/en-gb/announcements/ft-sets-the-agenda-with-new-brand-platform/ (archived at https://perma.cc/37PB-A74X)

5 Edelman (2019) https://www.edelman.com/news-awards/2019-institutional-investor-trust (archived at https://perma.cc/7K84-X99F)

6 Elkington, J (1997) *Cannibals with Forks: The triple bottom line of the 21st century*, Capstone, Oxford

7 Boynton, A (2015) Unilever's Paul Polman: CEOs can't be slaves to shareholders, *Forbes*, https://www.forbes.com/sites/andyboynton/2015/07/20/unilevers-paul-polman-ceos-cant-be-slaves-to-shareholders/ (archived at https://perma.cc/YJN6-TAKL)

8 Unilever (2018) https://www.unilever.com/Images/uslp-performance-summary-2018_tcm244-536032_en.pdf (archived at https://perma.cc/55W7-SPZZ)

9 Unilever (2014) *Scaling for Impact – Summary of progress 2014*, Unilever, London

10 Dietz, G and Hartog, D N D (2006) Measuring trust inside organizations, *Personnel Review*, 35 (5), pp 557–88

11 Hurley, R F (2006) The decision to trust, *Harvard Business Review*, 84 (9), pp 55–62

12 Zand, Z E (1997) *The Leadership Triad: Knowledge, trust and power*, Oxford University Press, Oxford

13 Rousseau, D M et al (1998) Not so different after all: A cross-discipline view of trust, *Academy of Management Review*, 23 (3), pp 393–404

14 Barney, J B and Hansen, M H (1994) Trustworthiness as a source of competitive advantage, *Strategic Management Journal*, 15 (S1), pp 175–90

15 Solomon, R C and Flores, F (2001) *Building Trust: Business, politics, relationships and life*, Oxford University Press, New York

16 Gabarro, J J (1978) The development of trust, influence, and expectations, in *Interpersonal Behavior: Communication and understanding in relationships*, ed A Athos and J Gabarro, Prentice Hall, p 303

17 Butler Jr, J K and Cantrell, R S (1984) A behavioral decision theory approach to modeling dyadic trust in superiors and subordinates, *Psychological Reports*, 55 (1), pp 19–28

18 Mishra, A K, Kramer, R and Tyler, T (1996) *Trust in Organizations: Frontiers of theory and research*, Sage, Thousand Oaks, CA

19 Burke, C S et al (2007) Trust in leadership: a multi-level review and integration, *The Leadership Quarterly*, **18** (6), pp 606–32

20 Donaldson, T and Preston, L E (1995) The stakeholder theory of the corporation: concepts, evidence, and implications, *Academy of Management Review*, **20** (1), pp 65–91

21 Block, P (1993) *Stewardship: Choosing service over self-interest*, Berrett-Koehler Publishers, Oakland, CA

22 Whitener, E M et al (1998) Managers as initiators of trust: an exchange relationship framework for understanding managerial trustworthy behaviour, *Academy of Management Review*, **23** (3), pp 513–30

23 Davis, J H, Schoorman, F D and Donaldson, L (1997) Toward a stewardship theory of management, *Academy of Management Review*, **22** (1), pp 20–47

24 Fukuyama, F (1995) *Trust: The social virtues and the creation of prosperity*, Free Press, New York

25 Accenture (2018) The Bottom Line on Trust, https://www.accenture.com/gb-en/insights/strategy/trust-in-business (archived at https://perma.cc/D79A-6N7P)

PART TWO

The nine habits that inspire results, relationships and reputation

Making a habit out of trustworthiness

At this stage in our journey I hope that I have answered the following questions:

- How is the purpose of business changing in a red pill world (single bottom line to triple bottom line)?
- What are the implications of this shift for the role of the executive leader (untrustworthy agent to trusted steward)?
- What is trust and how does it relate to trustworthiness?
- What are the three pillars that inspire trust (ability, integrity, benevolence)?

We have covered the theory of the three pillar model but everything that goes before begs a new question: How do I *do* trustworthiness? I mentioned in the Introduction that I intend to bridge the academic and the practical. The next three chapters focus on the practicalities of becoming proficient at inspiring trust. We are aiming beyond the goal of understanding this intellectually to applying it successfully and consistently in an executive leadership role. As a coach, I am interested in helping leaders be more effective rather than more knowledgeable. Sometimes gaining new knowledge is part of the formula that gets us from A to B, but it is rarely the full answer. As Einstein quipped, 'In theory, theory and practice are the same. In practice, they are not.' Consider the great books you have read and the excellent training courses you have attended. How many of them entertained you rather than changed you? If we wish to go beyond corporate entertainment then we have to commit to the hard yards of executive practice. However, even more than this, we have first to believe that it is possible to change at all.

All the CEOs I interviewed were asked the question, 'How do you build trustworthiness?' One of them replied, 'I am not sure this is the right question because I don't think you can build trustworthiness in people. You either have it or you don't and so we test for it when we recruit people into the business.' I am sure other executive leaders would have a similar perspective. Can you really build integrity into someone or is it a fixed trait of character that defies further development? This argument reminds me of Churchill's famous words about optimism: 'I suppose I am an optimist; there seems little point in being anything else.' So my glib answer to those who believe that trustworthiness is a fixed character trait would be: 'I suppose I believe that anyone can grow and change in profound ways; as a leader there seems little point in believing anything else.'

Dr Carole Dweck of Stanford University provides a more rigorous assessment of this question in her book *Mindset: The new psychology of success*.[1] Dr Dweck has spent decades studying achievement and success in students. She has concluded that we have one of two mindsets at any point in time: growth or fixed. Someone with a fixed mindset believes that talents and traits are fixed and unchangeable. They believe that if someone is not good at something there is no point in trying harder as their ability will not change. This mindset gets in the way of learning, since challenges are seen as threatening. In contrast, people with a growth mindset believe that abilities and talents are cultivated through effort. People with this attitude welcome a challenge and they create an inner resilience in the face of obstacles. Based on her research, Dr Dweck concludes that 'the more we know that basic human abilities can be grown, the more it becomes a basic human right for all kids and all adults to live in environments that create that growth'.

These coming chapters assume a growth mindset. They assume that each of the three pillars of trust is like a muscle that can be targeted with specific exercises and made strong through repetition and practice. This does not mean it is easy to build trustworthiness, in the same way that it is not easy to run a marathon, but it does mean it is possible. It also reveals that the key to success is not an innate ability but superlative motivation. As Durant said of Aristotle, 'We are what we repeatedly do. Excellence is not an act, it is a habit.' If you know someone who has given up smoking then you know that it is often hard to change a habit, but it is not impossible. New habits come from repetition and practice. Repetition and practice. Repetition and practice. And just as Covey had his seven habits of effectiveness,[2] I will offer you the nine leadership habits of trust. Nine habits that inspire results, relationships and reputation.

I did not dream up these Nine Habits over a glass of red wine; they are the product of six years of research at Aston Business School. I wanted to offer the business world an academically rigorous answer to the question, 'How do I do trust?' A solution that could stand the test of time. My research involved interviewing over 50 cross-sector, international CEOs and then surveying over 500 board-level leaders in the UK. The first qualitative phase of the study used the technique of thematic analysis to identify the leadership behaviours that CEOs felt were most likely to inspire trust. In the second quantitative phase, these behaviours were used to create a new 'Nine Habits' measurement tool and this was verified as reliable and consistent in measuring trust. In the final phase, the Nine Habits of Trust model was used to test the extent to which CEO and senior team leadership behaviour was a strong predictor of organizational trust. It was found there was a high correlation between leadership teams who demonstrate the Nine Habits of Trust and organizations with high-trust cultures. Therefore, the research supported the notion that the more senior you are in the organization, the more important are your own leadership habits in impacting the wider culture. First, we make our habits and then our habits make us! Paying attention to our trust-building habits is one of our most important leadership responsibilities

A habit is an accumulation of choices. If you want to change a habit then you have to start making different choices. To change a habit is an act of pure will, which is why it relies upon exceptional motivation. So are you ready to choose again, you trusted executives of tomorrow, because many of us have been leaning on that pillar of authority more than we realized? Do you have the will to change the habits of your trustworthiness and so thrive in the red pill world? If the answer is 'yes' then Figure II.1 shows the nine choices I will be challenging you to make. Three habits each for the pillars of ability, integrity and benevolence.

FIGURE II.1   The Nine Habits of Trust

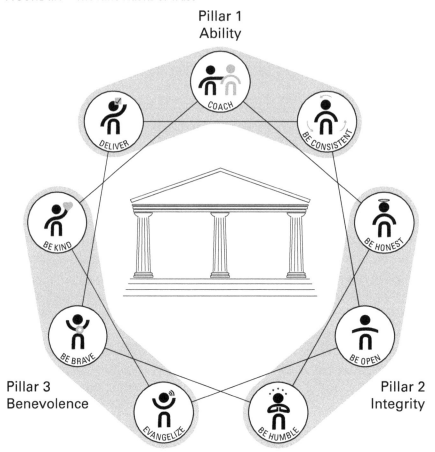

Three habits focused on building your ability:

Habit No.1: Choosing to deliver

This habit involves getting the job done on time, on budget and to the right level of satisfaction for the customer. If you can't deliver then it will be hard to trust you. Habit No.1 is the passport into the rest of the trust game.

Habit No.2: Choosing to coach

Coaching is being able to teach others to deliver through sharing your knowledge and developing their skills. This habit involves the skills of listening, asking powerful questions and empowering others.

Habit No.3: Choosing to be consistent

Inconsistency is a trust killer. If you deliver 99 days out of 100 and then it all falls apart on the 100th day, it will be the 100th day that people remember. Consistency isn't sexy or glamorous, but it's core to trustworthiness.

Three habits focused on building your integrity:

Habit No.4: Choosing to be honest

The bar on honesty is rising all the time. Any transgression can severely damage your reputation. People are watching 24/7, looking for cracks in the honesty habit, whether it's in your business life or your personal life.

Habit No.5: Choosing to be open

Being open is about having transparent communication, being clear about why you're doing what you're doing. It's also about showing vulnerability and being able to own up to your shortcomings and mistakes.

Habit No.6 Choosing to be humble

Humble leaders admit their part in failures, not seeking to claim all of the glory and putting the company and team ahead of themselves. This habit will help others feel like they work with you, not for you.

Three habits focused on building your benevolence:

Habit No.7: Choosing to evangelize

Leaders who exercise this habit set a positive tone and inspire confidence in others. They have the unwavering belief that the mission will be successful and they share this message with the team and with the wider stakeholders.

Habit No.8: Choosing to be brave

Do you have the moral courage to stick your neck out and to stand up for what you believe in? This is the type of bravery that builds trust when people know that you will do the right thing, even if it could have negative personal consequences.

Habit No.9: Choosing to be kind

An act of kindness takes an instant of time but requires great thought. Saying 'well done' and 'thank you' can have a dramatic effect on the morale and well-being of staff. Random acts of kindness, especially when they are unexpected, can instantly change people's attitudes in a positive way.

There are some words in these Nine Habits that will be familiar to executive leaders; words such as deliver, coach, be honest, be brave, be consistent. There also some words that might sit less easily with you if you come from the blue pill world; words such as be humble, be kind, be open. Probably the most surprising word to see in a business context is 'evangelize'. Often considered to be a religious habit, to evangelize is to 'spread the good news' and is increasingly being referred to as a broader leadership capability in business.[3]

It is interesting to compare the habits of the untrustworthy agent of the 'blue pill' world with these Nine Habits of the trusted 'red pill' steward. Table II.1 summarizes the key differences.

TABLE II.1   Comparison of the habits of stewards and agents

Steward Habit	Agent Habit	Supporting Comments
Deliver	Deliver	Business is a performance sport. We always had to deliver and we still need to deliver. This habit does not change.
Coach	Tell	In the 'blue pill' world, I told you what to do with my bigger brain. In the 'red pill' world people don't want to be told what to do, so we need to coach them by asking questions, listening and empowering.
Be Consistent	Be Unpredictable	In the 'blue pill' world, unpredictable leaders kept us on our toes where fear was the glue of life, but nothing destroys trust as quickly as unpredictability of behaviour. If I don't know where I stand in relation to you, I will not trust you.
Be Honest	Be Expedient	In a world where nothing can be hidden the bar on honesty is ruthlessly high. What used to be tolerated as gamesmanship, spin, exaggeration is no longer acceptable.

TABLE II.1   *continued*

Steward Habit	Agent Habit	Supporting Comments
Be Open	Be Guarded	'Blue pill' alpha males were taught never to show weakness. Diverse 'red pill' stewards will show their full, vulnerable selves at the right time and in the right place to inspire trust.
Be Humble	Be Arrogant	In the 'blue pill' world, you could get away with being arrogant so long as you were successful. In the 'red pill' world, we expect leaders to be on the same level as us regardless of how successful they are.
Evangelize	Manipulate	The charismatic leaders of the 'blue pill' era knew how to manipulate others to achieve short term, singular outcomes. Trusted stewards inspire others through a passionate vision that delivers holistic, sustainable goals.
Be Brave	Self-Serve	Trusted stewards show moral bravery to speak out for the wider good. Untrustworthy agents sacrifice others to pursue personal gain.
Be Kind	Be Negligent	Trusted stewards know that kindness is the purple dye of leadership – one drop and it changes the whole complexion of a situation. Untrustworthy agents were taught that there is no place for kindness in the workplace.

EXERCISE

Assess the following celebrity leaders against the Nine Habits of Trust. For each leader, identify their two strongest habits and their weakest habit:

- Donald Trump.
- Steve Jobs.
- Mother Teresa.
- Oprah Winfrey.

Closer to home, think of the leader in your career that has most inspired you. Which of the Nine Habits did they master? Did they have a habit that was an Achilles heel when it came to building trust?

Finally, think of a company brand that you admire. How would you assess that brand against the Nine Habits of Trust? Which habits have they successfully developed into cultural traits and values?

In the next three chapters we explore each of these Nine Habits in detail using case studies, relevant psychological models, personal anecdotes and excerpts from interviews with practising CEOs. At the end of each chapter, I will ask you to assess your habits using a simple set of questionnaires; identifying your strengths and challenging you to develop a practical plan to improve your performance in areas where there is more work to do. Ultimately, you will be able to use the results of the questionnaires to gauge your trustworthiness quotient (TQ). Three pillars. Nine leadership habits. The theory is simple; now let's get down to practice.

Endnotes

1 Dweck, C (2006) *Mindset: The new psychology of success*, Random House, New York

2 Covey, S (1989) *The Seven Habits of Highly Successful People*, Fireside/Simon & Schuster, New York

3 Kawasaki, G (2015) Managing yourself: The art of evangelism, *Harvard Business Review*, **93** (5), pp 108–11

03

Pillar 1: Habits of ability

 Choosing to deliver

First things first. I am going to focus later upon a range of soft skills in the habits of trustworthiness, but I want to start with a hard skill – delivering superlative results. It's appropriate to begin with delivering results because without this fundamental habit it is unlikely that you will get a pass to the next stage of the executive leadership game. We are in the performance business and performance is measured by achieving challenging goals; these may be triple bottom line goals, but they are still results-focused goals. Consistently, the CEOs I interviewed highlighted this habit:

'Not being late, not going over budget, not moving commercials around on the hop.'

'Don't let your customer down.'

'There is always a distrust of government because they make promises that they can't deliver and many businesses are the same.'

'McKinsey don't just go the extra mile; they go the extra 1,000 miles.'

'The ultimate arbiter is the customer because they have choice. If they expect x and you deliver y then you have failed. If you deliver x+ you have succeeded.'

We know all of this and yet so often we don't do it. We over-promise and we under-deliver. We walk out of meetings where there has been no commitment to take action. We pass the buck, we slope our shoulders and we hope that no one will notice. When I started my career at British Gas, I was mentored by a front-line supervisor who was responsible for following up customer enquiries. At the end of the first week of shadowing him, he let me into a secret. He opened his bottom desk drawer and pulled out a massive wad of outstanding customer enquiry sheets. Quietly, he dealt the sheets into two neat piles. The first pile he placed gently into the bin and the second pile he put back in the drawer. Then he turned to me and said, 'That's how I prioritize my work.' Each week he threw away 50 per cent of the enquiries without the blink of an eye! As a young graduate trainee, I was astounded and yet it was only the first of many episodes in my career when I encountered alarming acts of promise-breaking, excuse-making, casual neglect of customer expectations and general delivery malaise.

According to Loehr *et al*, 'accountability is protection from our infinite capacity for self-deception'.[1] And a lack of accountability destroys trustworthiness like a bout of the plague. In Patrick Lencioni's impactful work on the five dysfunctions of a team, five traps typically undermine the performance of management teams.[2] The fourth trap he terms 'avoidance of accountability'. At a recent conference event, I sat in a room of 250 CEOs who completed a self-assessment exercise to identify which of Lencioni's five dysfunctions were most prevalent in their management teams. When the speaker came to request a show of hands for those CEOs who felt 'avoidance of accountability' was their most pressing issue, it was like being back in the classroom when the teacher asks the pupils, 'Who wants a sweet?' So many hands shot up that the speaker stopped counting and resigned himself to saying, 'I've done this exercise with countless teams all round the world these past four years and it is always avoidance of accountability that is a team's most common Achilles heel.' Every time you don't do what you say you are going to do, you undermine your trustworthiness and you invite others to do the same.

So how do we build accountability into ourselves and those around us? How do we get a reputation for delivering results and exceeding expectations? The habit of 'choosing to deliver' involves three crucial steps:

1 Be careful when making promises.
2 Have a system that manages the execution and delegation of tasks.
3 Exceed expectations to generate a 'wow' factor.

1. Be careful when making promises

It starts with being extremely careful when we make promises. And we make a promise every time we say we are going to do something. An honest 'No,

I'm too busy right now' is preferable to a half-hearted 'Yes, I'll have a look at that'. For example, at the end of each of my executive coaching sessions I draw up a list of the actions that the executive leader has agreed to take and I ask the question, 'On a scale of 0 to 10, how committed are you to taking this action?' My experience tells me that unless the leader replies with a minimum of an '8' then the action is unlikely to be completed and it is best scrubbed off the list. Similarly, at the end of our Trusted Executive Fellowship Board meetings each member is asked to write down on the flipchart the one action that they are willing to be held accountable for by the rest of the group; you know that those actions are most likely to be completed because the member has made a public promise in front of respected peers.

On a bigger scale, when we agree to a performance target we are making a promise. When we sign a new contract with a customer or supplier we are making a promise. When we make a forecast of future earnings to the City we are making a promise. The consequences of breaking these promises are significant, not just in terms of commercial outcomes, but also in terms of trustworthiness. One company chairman described it thus:

> The finance director never kept his promises. He would promise to pay something and it wouldn't happen. Initially, there was a loss of confidence in the individual but it translated eventually into a loss of confidence in the organization as a whole and it infected everyone who was in it. In many respects, that one individual destroyed that business.

2. Have a system that manages the execution and delegation of tasks

Once we have made a careful promise then we need a system for both execution and delegation. This is an issue of discipline. I do not intend to delve into the detail of all the task management systems that are available and their relative merits. I simply want to ask if you have a technology-enabled system for the management of your promises (aka a 'to do list') and your delegated promises. Some of my clients use an array of Excel spreadsheets, some use the latest smartphone apps like Trello, some appear to be doing some advanced programming in Outlook and others swear by Evernote as the rock that holds their life together. The point is that they have a system that works for them and they use technology to make that system robust and efficient. For those who need to delve deeper into this aspect of choosing to deliver, I recommend David Allen's classic text *Getting Things Done: The art of stress-free productivity*.[3]

3. Exceed expectations to generate a 'wow' factor

Finally, in choosing to deliver we are aiming to exceed rather than meet the expectations of our stakeholders. In the beginning, we made a careful promise and now we look to conclude the cycle by delivering the 'wow' factor. One of my colleagues, the outstanding motivational speaker Marcus Child, captures the need to strive for the 'wow' factor by using the following 'three circles of delivery' model – see Figure 3.1.

FIGURE 3.1   The three circles of delivery

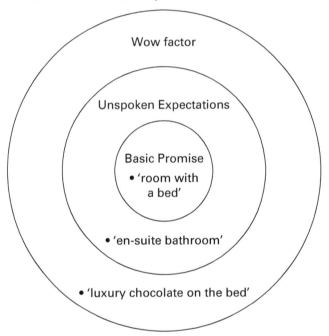

In this model, the inner circle represents the basic promise. If I am booking a hotel room then a basic promise is a room with a bed. The next circle represents the unspoken expectations. If I book a hotel room then I expect that there will be an en-suite bathroom though I may not specifically request it. The final circle represents the point where my expectations are exceeded and I experience the 'wow' factor. I walk into my hotel room, tired from a long day, and there on the bed is a small box of luxury chocolates. Now, clearly, if I walked into the room and there was no bed and no en-suite bathroom, just a small box of chocolates on the floor, then that is not going to deliver the 'wow' factor. Our basic promises and unspoken expectations must be consistently met before we can generate a 'wow' factor. Translating this model to the world of your personal trustworthiness, how can you 'wow' not just your customers but your management team, your suppliers and your local community? And a word of warning: remember that today's 'wow' factors are always tomorrow's 'unspoken expectations'. Choosing to deliver the 'wow' factor is a journey that will never end.

 ## Choosing to coach

When we have mastered the habit of choosing to deliver we can help others to also deliver through coaching. We achieve this partly by role-modelling the delivery skills ourselves, because those around us will learn from our example. This counts for a lot, but there are other aspects of choosing to coach that go beyond leading by example. I recall many years ago witnessing a vivid example of the case for coaching when leadership guru Graham Alexander asked for a volunteer from a room full of executives at the beginning of a course on coaching skills. Graham asked the volunteer to lie flat on the ground and invited another volunteer from the audience to 'tell' the first person how to get up. The audience collapsed into laughter as the person 'telling' repeatedly failed to make any impact with instructions such as 'push down on your right hand', 'bend your left elbow', 'roll over onto your side' and 'lift your knee to your waist'. It was like watching a drunken man in a suit play a game of 'Twister'. Finally, after 10 minutes of frustration and bodily contortions, Graham put the volunteers out of their misery by walking up and saying to the man on the floor, 'Do you know how to get up?' The man breathlessly replied, 'Yes, of course I do!' 'Well, get up then,' Graham concluded. And he did. In that brief exchange he showed the simple power of the core coaching skills: ask, listen, empower.[4]

In the red pill world it is relatively ineffective to tell other people what to do. This is partly because in a global, diverse, technology-enabled environment there are more and more situations in which the leader no longer has the expert knowledge and, partly, because the Generation Y knowledge workers on the receiving end of the 'telling' are not motivated by this style of leadership. It's a 'lose-lose' approach in most situations other than when there is a simple, urgent task that requires a specific, direct instruction. This is why, in the past 10 years, coaching has sprung into the mainstream agenda of leadership development. We have moved from a world where my job as a leader was to show you how clever I was to a world where I need to show you how clever you are and I do that by choosing to coach you. I do that through asking, listening and empowering.

'I have no great skills, I am only passionately curious' is another of my favourite lines from Einstein. Trustworthy leaders are passionately curious and they demonstrate this by asking lots of questions. Furthermore, the questions they ask are powerful ones: questions that dig deep and open up new lines of thinking. One of the models that helps us to ask powerful questions is known as Bateson's logical levels (see Figure 3.2).

FIGURE 3.2   Logical levels

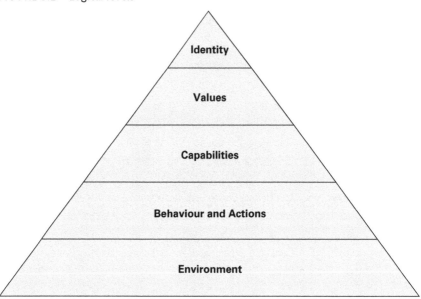

If we ask questions at the higher levels of the hierarchy then these require more brain power to answer than those at lower levels. We have to dig deeper when the focus of the question shifts from issues of environment and behaviour to issues of capabilities, values and identity. While it is often more challenging to work at the higher logical levels, it is also more powerful, because rewiring the brain at the level of identity triggers rewiring at all the lower levels too. Hence, when it comes to asking questions, questions that challenge us to think about our values and identity are inherently more powerful than questions that ask us to think about environment and behaviour. For example, an annual performance review is an excellent opportunity for a leader to coach. In such a discussion, I can ask many questions and some will be more powerful than others. Consider the following questions and, as you read them, gauge their relative impact:

- Environment – 'What has been happening in your team this past year?'
- Behaviour – 'How did you handle the leadership challenge in winning back your number one account?'
- Capability – 'What leadership competencies do you feel are critical for you to develop?'
- Values – 'What are your core beliefs about leadership?'
- Identity – 'Who are you as a leader?'

Bateson's model helps us think about the type of questions that we ask as executive leaders. Whether it be with our staff, our customers, our board peers or our shareholders, the frequency and type of questions we ask will be a crucial component of choosing to coach. As David Marquet puts it: 'Bosses get people to do, leaders get people to think'[5] and they do this by asking great questions. Yet asking is only half the picture, because there is no point in asking unless we then choose to listen.

Similar to the art of asking questions, there are many levels at which we can listen. In her book *Co-Active Coaching*,[6] Laura Whitworth dedicates a whole chapter to listening and introduces three levels of listening:

Level I – internal listening

Level II – focused listening

Level III – global listening

At level I, we are preoccupied with our own internal dialogue; our thoughts, our feelings and our opinions. At level II, we have shifted the focus to the other person and we are focusing upon their thoughts, feelings and opinions, together with how they are speaking in terms of tone, rhythm and body language. At level III, Whitworth describes global listening as follows:

> At level III, you listen as though you and [the other person] were at the centre of the universe receiving information from everywhere at once. It is as though you were surrounded by a force field that contains you, the [other person] and the space of knowing. If level II is hard-wired then level III is like a radio field.

Imagine you are in a board meeting. One of your colleagues, Julie, is presenting the new digital marketing strategy for the business. You are listening at level I. Your head is full of internal chatter: 'I wonder how my PA is getting on with organizing my diary for the week', 'My back is still causing me pain', 'I'm feeling really bored with this meeting'. Suddenly, you hear your colleague say, 'Our target NPS score really should be above 50, but is languishing at 45.' You lean forward and ask a question: 'Julie, can you just tell me what NPS is, please?' You switch from level I to level II listening. As your colleague answers your question, you notice that she appears nervous and her hands are shaking. She is speaking fast. You cannot understand the answer because it is full of jargon. Your intuition is telling you that something does not fit. You switch from level II to level III listening. As you concentrate further, it comes to you in a flash: 'Hang on a moment, Julie, something is not right here. You don't seem your normal self today. Are you ok?' At this, your colleague puts down her papers and says, 'I've been trying to struggle on, but I've just heard some bad news about my mother's health.' 'That's fine,' you reply. 'Get yourself home. We can review this strategy at another time.'

That is what we mean by listening at three different levels. Each level is appropriate and relevant depending upon the situation. However, we need to know at which level we are listening and have the flexibility to switch levels if required.

We have asked and we have listened and now we can choose to empower. Empowerment is a well-established topic in leadership circles and it intertwines with the notion of belief. Do I believe in you? Do I *really* believe in you? Do I believe in you more than you believe in yourself? When you encounter empowerment on this scale you tend to remember it because it is rare. The people who believe in you to this extent are special people. In my experience, the world of business can learn a lot about empowerment from the world of Olympic sport.

CASE STUDY
Alan Campbell: Olympic medallist rower

One of the most outrageous acts of empowerment I have witnessed occurred between my ex-business partner, Bill Barry, and a novice rower, Alan Campbell, back in 2002. Bill is an Olympic silver medallist, ex-CEO of an international advertising agency and coach to many Olympic rowers. He has been there and done it. One summer evening he was invited to his local 'Tideway Scullers' rowing club in London to watch a raw, young talent rowing on the Thames. Alan Campbell was that raw talent and, back in those days, Alan was an overweight, uncoordinated 18-year-old. Once he had completed the training session, Alan bounded up the riverbank to Bill and introduced himself. 'What is your goal?' Bill asked him. 'To win an Olympic medal' was the impulsive reply. At this point Bill would have been wholly within his rights to laugh off the suggestion and dismiss the callow young man back to his native Northern Ireland. In business terms, it was akin to a teenage apprentice marching into the global CEO's office and demanding a place on the board. However, after Alan had come out with his preposterous ambition that evening, Bill recalled that he saw a strange determination in Alan's eyes so he took him at his word and said, 'Well, if you want to win an Olympic medal, I'll be your coach and I need you to lose 15 kg in weight in the next four months.' Their coaching journey began that day and ended 10 years later on 3 August 2012 when Alan won the bronze medal in the single scull final of the London Olympics – the first single scull medal Team GB had achieved in that event for 84 years. Bill believed in Alan at a time when many others would not have done. That belief empowered Alan and inspired him to commit 110 per cent to his goal.

I remember pivotal moments of empowerment in my business career. At the age of 25, I was appointed by Graham Nye of British Gas as the youngest senior manager in the region. At 33, Iain Barker, CEO of Team 121 Ltd, asked me to set up the company's first international subsidiary in Oslo. At 46, Nicholas Brealey granted me my first book publishing contract. We remember these people's names because they backed us to be more than we thought we were and they were brave to take a risk on our unrealized potential. Who believes in you? And who do you believe in? These are important questions for the trustworthy leader who chooses to coach.

 ## Choosing to be consistent

Our final habit of ability is choosing to be consistent in your behaviours. Gandhi said that 'happiness is when what you think, what you say and what you do are in harmony'. When others experience you as consistent, reliable and predictable it brings happiness on the inside, and trustworthiness on the outside. In many ways, choosing to be consistent is the least glamorous of all the nine leadership habits, yet it is also the habit that underpins all the others. You can be kind for 99 days out of 100, but if you are cruel on the hundredth day that is the day that people will remember. You can be honest 99 days out of 100, but if you lie on the hundredth day that is the day people will remember. And in sport as well as in business, we know that you're only as good as your last result. In the red pill world, consistency counts.

Contrast this with life in the blue pill world. I recall working for leaders who saw it as their job to be deliberately unpredictable and inconsistent in their behaviour. The blue pill thinking was that you needed to 'keep people on their toes'; if you let them relax then we'd all be 'going to hell in a hand cart'. It was always exciting working for these leaders, but their approach destroyed trust because nobody knew where they stood. When you don't know where you stand you get nervous and when you get nervous you start to spend a lot of time and energy playing political games; it's a shocking waste of talent. One CEO I spoke to likened inconsistent leaders to the hyperactive character Tigger in A A Milne's *Winnie the Pooh*: 'Nobody ever trusted anyone who was not consistent. "Tigger" bosses are the worst to work for: they may be enthusiastic but everyone is always off-balance around them.' It takes immense self-confidence to be consistent because it means that you are not blown around by shifting political winds. You have an inner compass that guides your behaviour irrespective of the circumstances in which you find yourself. That internal compass is a set of values. As Vistage speaker Glen Daly stresses: 'Values are the small number of fundamental and lasting principles that guide all aspects of our behaviour'. The habit of choosing to be consistent is the habit of living by your values.

So do you know what your values are? Do you live by them? Does your company know what its values are? Does it live by them? In my early days as an executive coach, I learnt a remarkable and simple exercise that enabled me to define my values. I have since conducted this exercise many times with my clients and it consistently delivers the goods. Often, people choose their values from a checklist. However, this creates the risk that the values are judged before being chosen. For example, people might dismiss a value of 'beauty' as being too superficial or choose a value of 'honesty' because it is a value they think they should have rather than one that genuinely inspires them.

EXERCISE

The following exercise attempts to by-pass this judgement of values by asking you to describe your values through 'real life' stories of personal fulfilment and despair. In these situations, values will either have been honoured or discounted and personal 'story-telling' helps these values to emerge via a non-judgmental process:

- Identify three peak moments when life felt perfect, fulfilled and 'in the flow'. Relive these experiences and recount them to a trusted colleague. Explore the details of the moment. What was happening? Who was there? What did people say? What did you see? What did you feel? What made it special? What else do you remember about it?

- Ask the colleague to play back what he or she heard about the experience and which words had most impact and energy for him or her. What values do you both think were being honoured in this experience? Choose a maximum of four values.

- Next identify three moments of despair when life felt empty, blocked and frustrating. Repeat the above steps for these experiences. Working with the colleague to identify the values you were ignoring during these times. As before, choose a maximum of four values.

- Combine the two lists of values and start to assess the priority of each by asking yourself the question: 'If my house was burning down and my values were in the house, which value would I take with me first?' And which one next... and so forth.

- After the discussion, write down your values in order of priority and add a couple of sentences to each that describes them in more detail. There should be a maximum of eight values on your list.

This exercise can also be carried out for a team or an organization by reviewing the relevant history and identifying the same high and low points. It is those moments when emotions are running strong that reveal the true values of an individual, a team or an organization as opposed to the textbook values that our logical brains would suggest.

What do we do with our set of values once we have identified them? They are no use as a dry set of words that are reeled out at annual performance appraisals and business retreats. We have to live by our values if they are to demonstrate our consistency. Living by our values means converting them into a decision-making tool. Thankfully, there are many ways to do this and I will share three simple tools that drive values into the heart of decision making.

First, at the personal level, I have had a weekly habit for the past 12 years where I take 10 minutes on a Sunday evening, I pull up my Evernote app and I open the note titled 'How I honoured my values this week'. In this note I see the following list of values:

- challenge;
- variety;
- sharing;
- freedom;
- flair;
- care;
- courage;
- fun.

I then look at my diary for the week and I write down what I am going to do that week to live out each value. For example, I might be speaking at an international conference and that would tag the values of challenge, sharing, flair and courage. I might be writing on a weekday and popping out to the gym over lunch, which honours my values of freedom, fun and variety. Through this weekly routine, I become aware of which values I honoured and which I squeezed. I then make decisions about my future commitments to keep them in balance. I have found this a powerful tool for living out my values at a personal level.

FIGURE 3.3   Values/results matrix

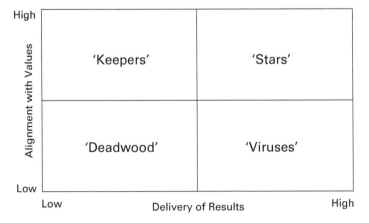

At the level of the team or organization, another proven tool for converting values into a decision-making tool is the 2 × 2 matrix shown in Figure 3.3.[7] This grid takes two of the habits of trustworthiness and plots them against each other. On one axis we have the habit of delivering results and on the other we have the habit of consistent behaviours, as measured by alignment with the company values. Members of a team can be plotted onto this grid to reveal who are the 'stars' (high values fit, high results), 'keepers' (high values fit, low results), 'deadwood' (low values fit, low results) and 'viruses' (low values fit, high results). Typically, it is the team members who are in the virus box that create a dilemma for leaders. On the public stage, we see this played out in sports teams where the maverick but hugely talented superstar delivers moments of magic on the sports field while routinely destroying trust in the dressing room due to a lack of alignment with the team's values. Whether your sport of choice is cricket, baseball, football or ice hockey, I am sure that you could quickly place some high-profile names in the 'virus' box of your chosen team. Executive leaders who choose to be consistent will live by their values and therefore will treat low values performers just as harshly as they treat low results performers. In so doing, they demonstrate the confidence to suffer the loss of short-term results for the longer-term sustainable benefit of building trustworthiness with staff, customers and other stakeholders. As you plot your own team members onto the grid to identify your own 'viruses', you will quickly find out whether you are choosing to make decisions based on your values or merely talking about them.

Finally, we can live by our values in a team setting by appointing someone to monitor and feed back on our performance. For example, in our monthly Trusted Executive Fellowship Board meetings, one of the CEO members is asked to play the role of 'Nine Habits guardian' for the day. The role of the Nine Habits guardian is to note during the day specific behaviours in the group that honour the habits and those that do not; they hold the group accountable to living the values. At the end of the meeting, the Nine Habits guardian plays back his or her findings. Example comments might be:

> 'I noticed that Jane completed all the actions she committed to at the previous meeting and I thought this was a good example of our trust habit of delivery.'

> 'I noticed that when our guest arrived, Peter immediately got up, made his chair available and offered the guest a drink. I am not sure I am always as quick to do that and it made me think about Habit No.9 – choosing to be kind – and Habit No.3 – choosing to be consistent.'

'The energy dropped after lunch, but it was great to see that Martin pulled us out of that dip by sharing his company's inspiring triple bottom line vision. I thought that was a great example of Habit No.7 – choosing to evangelize.'

Through this monthly routine we keep the Nine Habits alive in the group and we progressively learn the practical behaviours that make the habits concrete and tangible. New members are quickly caught up in this culture because they are exposed to practical experiences and specific feedback rather than vague PowerPoint-based aspirations.

In summary, choosing to be consistent involves first identifying our values and then converting these into a variety of decision-making tools for use by individuals, teams and organizations. The good news is that over time it becomes second nature to make values-based decisions because it becomes a habit. As well as building our reputation for trustworthiness with others, this habit reduces stress for ourselves by simplifying the decision-making process. We start to experience the benefit that Roy Disney commented upon when he said, 'It is not hard to make decisions when you know what your values are.' A final word for anyone who thinks that values-driven leadership is boring: it can be, but not if one of your values is fun!

DO HB CHECK SELF-ASSESSMENT

We have covered the first pillar of trustworthiness and the three habits of ability. At this stage it is worth pausing to consolidate our understanding. As I stressed at the beginning of the chapter, becoming a trusted executive is about building new leadership habits. It helps us build habits if we have simple reminders and tools to structure our learning. Miller's Law[8,9] states that we can only hold 7 +/– 2 pieces of information in our working memory at any point in time. Since nine habits is on the upper limit of Miller's Law it is helpful to create a mnemonic to help us quickly remember all nine habits. My mnemonic for the nine habits is 'DO HB CHECK' where the letters stand for each of the habits as follows:

D – deliver
O – open

H – humble
B – brave

C – coach
H – honesty
E – evangelize
C – consistency
K – kindness

The 'DO HB CHECK' phrase also allows us to introduce a self-assessment tool for use after we have introduced each set of three habits. Listed in Table 3.1 are the habits of ability together with three behaviours under each habit. Please take a moment to assess yourself against each of these behaviours. If you are working through this book with colleagues, you can also gain their perspectives and use these perceptions to establish your strengths and areas for development for the habits of ability.

TABLE 3.1   DO HB CHECK self-assessment: habits of ability

	Never	Rarely	Occasionally	Frequently	Always
I am careful when making promises					
I use a proven system for tracking the execution and delegation of tasks					
I go above and beyond what is expected in my key stakeholder relationships					
I listen to others more than I talk to them					
I ask questions of everyone I meet					
I believe in people's potential more than they believe in it themselves					

TABLE 3.1 *continued*

	Never	Rarely	Occasionally	Frequently	Always
I act consistently despite changing circumstances					
I make decisions based on my personal values					
I role-model our organizational values on a consistent basis					

CEO coaching session – habits of ability

The following transcript has been created to bring to life the points raised in the chapter. There are many ways to develop the habits of ability. One of these is through working with an executive coach. The intention of featuring this dialogue between coach and CEO is to give you a detailed example of how the habits of ability can be developed amidst the day-to-day intensity of an executive leadership role.

In this coaching scenario, the coachee, Rob, is the CEO of a property services company. Rob has been in the post for almost three years. He was originally recruited to the role from outside the company to turn round its performance. Rob has engaged a coach to work with him on a programme of nine two-hour face-to-face coaching sessions. This transcript is from session six of the programme. While the example below is informed by my experience of working with CEOs, it is not based on any real person or actual event.

Coach: Hi Rob, what topic would you like to work on today?

Rob: Well, I've been reading your book and thinking about the habits of ability: delivering results, coaching others and being consistent. I asked my team to complete the DO HB CHECK assessment at the end of the chapter and this has highlighted that my team regard me as a 'Tigger' boss. It seems they think that I am not consistent and that I jump around from one day to the next. This has come as a bit of a shock to me.

Coach: How come it was a shock?

Rob: No one has ever mentioned this before, but then I suppose most of the 360 degree feedback surveys I have completed did not check for consistency; they were more focused on broader leadership skills such as strategic thinking, building relationships and client focus. In fact, I have previously been praised for my decisiveness and my ability to react quickly to changing circumstances. I've previously thought that my spontaneous, fast-paced style built trust because I was making things happen.

Coach: Yes, I guess it demonstrates your ability to deliver.

Rob: I thrive in a crisis. I loved it a couple of years ago when we were turning round this business. Every day there were critical decisions to make and we had to move quickly to rescue the situation. Now, the business is on a much stronger footing, the numbers are looking good and... well... no... it's all fine.

Coach: The numbers are looking good and...

Rob: To be honest, I'm getting bored. I come in on a Monday morning and it's all running smoothly. I sit here in this office twiddling my thumbs and I get to the point where I think I better stir things up a bit, because I'm worried that the team is getting complacent. Last week, I tore a strip off Simon because we had a customer complaint and I thought, 'There you go. That's how it starts. You need to jump on this before things get any worse'.

Coach: But I thought the business had just posted its best month and your customer satisfaction scores were in the top 10 per cent of your industry?

Rob: Yes, that's right. On reflection, I over-reacted with Simon. I jumped to a conclusion and started making waves. He didn't take it well at all. He told me that 'it was becoming an issue of trust', which I didn't fully understand at the time.

Coach: Rob, what is the biggest challenge in your business right now? We know it's not sales or customer satisfaction. What is it?

Rob: Like I said, things are going well. I'm not sure we have a 'biggest challenge'.

Coach: You know I'm not going to accept that as an answer. What's your biggest challenge right now?

Rob: Ok. Let me think... Julie resigned last month and that was a big disappointment on two fronts. We didn't want to lose her and she's gone to one of our competitors as their new director of marketing. Three months ago, we also lost Farhan who was one of our high potential account managers. It's not a crisis, but I wouldn't want us to lose any more people in our sales and marketing team. That's probably the biggest risk to us right now.

Coach: And how does your perceived lack of consistency play into that risk?

Rob: Ok, I see where you are going with this. It's a fair cop. In fact, Julie mentioned in her exit interview that she was sick and tired of all the chopping and changing in the company. She said it undermined her confidence and that she didn't know where she stood from one day to the next. She didn't mention me by name, but I suppose I can join the dots, particularly now that I have had this other feedback from the rest of the team.

Coach: Good. So what are you going to do about it?

Rob: You're the coach. You tell me!

Coach: Do you remember that exercise we completed at the beginning of the coaching programme on your values?

Rob: Yes, I do and I know you talk about it in your book when it comes to developing the habit of consistency. That exercise helped me a lot at the time, but I'm not sure how it could help me now.

Coach: Remind me what your values are.

Rob: Spontaneity, action, variety, loyalty and collaboration.

Coach: Ok. So when you get bored because things are going so well, what do you think is going on?

Rob: I'm getting bored because my values of spontaneity and action are getting squeezed. It's like the ship has set sail: we've set the right course and I'm stood on the deck as the captain staring at the sea and wondering what to do next. So I just shout, 'Man the rigging!' as loudly as I can. Everybody jumps, then they start running around. It's a bit chaotic, but I can tell you it sure gets the adrenalin pumping.

Coach: Sounds like great fun... until someone trips over the mainstay in the confusion and cartwheels overboard. Missing in action?

Rob: Yes, that would be First Officer Julie, wouldn't it?

Coach: That's right. Now, let's imagine just before you yelled 'Man the rigging!' you paused the film and checked in with each of your values. What would happen then?

Rob: I'd check in with the spontaneity and action values and realize that I was bored. I'd also check in with my values of loyalty and collaboration and realize that if I yell 'Man the rigging' I'll cause mayhem and that risks losing someone from the team and undermining everyone's trust in me. So that leaves me with variety.

Coach: How could your value of variety help you in that situation as you stand on deck staring out to sea?

Rob: Got it. I'll go down below deck and get the ship's cook to rustle up a hearty English breakfast!

Coach: Brilliant. Sounds like a spontaneous act that generates some action without risking the loyalty and collaboration of the crew. Now, let's bring it back to the real world of business. What's the equivalent of 'going down below and asking the ship's cook to rustle up a hearty English breakfast' in your role as CEO?

Rob: Unfortunately, we closed the staff canteen as part of my turnaround measures a couple of years ago but, seriously, I have been meaning to have a chat with one of our technology partners about how we take our digital media strategy to the next level. I feel that we are missing a trick there and the competition is stealing a march on us. I'd like to ask our partners to organize an initiative to look at best practice in this area and work with me directly to pull together a plan of action.

Coach: That's a great example. What else would honour those values without undermining the trust in your management team?

Rob: It makes me think of the habit of choosing to coach. It's one thing for me to bark orders to my team, but if I could get involved with them as a coach rather than as a boss then I could see that would build the trust rather than undermine it. So I could organize regular one-to-ones with my immediate team and treat these as coaching sessions in which I ask questions, listen and empower. I could imagine once I got into that then it would be an interesting new challenge.

Coach: Another great example. How does that feel as two initiatives to take forward before we next meet?

Rob: Great. I can get excited about that plan. It will reduce the risk of me getting bored, whilst keeping me out of the hair of others in my team who are doing a great job.

Coach: I'm hoping that you can see how your team will regard you as a more consistent leader if you honour your full set of values in this way. You don't have to become a different person; it's just a case of being aware of when you get the urge to yell 'Man the rigging' and seeing that as a warning sign. The antidote is to bite your lip and consider how you might honour your values of spontaneity and action in a different way; a way that doesn't undermine the trust you have built with the team by forever chopping and changing.

Rob: Yes, I get it. Let's review how I have got on with this when we next meet.

In summary, the dialogue shows how Rob worked on the habits of choosing to be consistent and choosing to coach. The coach used his values as an important resource, partly to understand what was happening for him as a leader and, partly, to create a way forward. The key learning for Rob was that he was at risk of over-playing his delivery strength. Without an immediate crisis to tackle, he was getting bored and his team were experiencing him as inconsistent and interfering. Trust was being undermined. Through raising his self-awareness, Rob gains clarity on the situation and commits to take action in two specific areas that have the potential to make a big difference, both to his own job satisfaction and the team's overall performance.

Endnotes

1   Loehr, J, Loehr, J E and Schwartz, T (2004) *The Power of Full Engagement: Managing energy, not time, is the key to high performance and personal renewal*, Simon and Schuster, New York

2   Lencioni, P (2006) *The Five Dysfunctions of a Team*, Wiley, Chichester

3   Allen, D (2002) *Getting Things Done: The art of stress-free productivity*, Penguin, Harmondsworth

4   Dilts, R (1990) *Changing Belief Systems with NLP, Vol 990*, Meta Publications Cupertino, CA

5 Marquet, L D (2013) *Turn the Ship Around! A true story of turning followers into leaders*, Portfolio

6 Whitworth, L (2007) *Co-active Coaching: New skills for coaching people toward success in work and life*, Davies-Black Publishing, Mountain View, CA

7 Cohen, D (2017) Who are the REAL stars in your organization? *Strategic Action Group*, https://www.sagltd.com/post/2017/07/13/who-are-the-real-stars-in-your-organization (archived at https://perma.cc/Q8U3-GXCJ)

8 Baddeley, A (1994) The magical number seven: Still magic after all these years? *Psychological Review*, **101** (2), pp 353–56

9 Miller, G A (1956) The magical number seven, plus or minus two, *Psychological Review*, **63** (2), p 81

04

Pillar 2: Habits of integrity

 Choosing to be honest

One of my earliest memories is of stealing. I must have been all of five years old at the time; clearly an early developer! My friend Simon and I both had Jonty West action dolls and we would proudly bring them into school each day; only Simon's Jonty West had a cowboy hat and mine did not. Children have a simplistic attitude to solving this type of problem. If you want it, you go and get it! So I took the hat and suddenly it was mine. The next day, our teacher, Miss Bell, addressed the class advising us that 'Simon's cowboy hat has gone missing. Does anyone know where it might be?' Now what was that strange sensation of burning heat in my cheeks? I found myself putting my hand up and saying that I thought I had seen the missing hat in the cloakroom. Miss Bell asked me to go and see if I could find it. So I shuffled off to the cloakroom, produced the hat from my pocket and stuck my hand down the back of an iron radiator. Then, turning to face the classroom, I thrust my hand in the air and cried 'I've found it!'. I thought I'd got away with it until my mum asked me one day, 'How come Simon doesn't invite you to his birthday parties anymore?'

Forty-five years on, I am no longer stealing cowboy hats, but I am still pondering on the habit of choosing to be honest. What does it mean for a trusted steward to be brutally honest? Where is the line between exaggeration and deceit? What is the difference between gamesmanship and cheating? How does today's healthy competition deteriorate into tomorrow's bad practice?

Sir David Brailsford, coach to Team GB cycling squad, explained the team's unprecedented medal haul at the 2016 Rio Olympics by citing the aggregation of marginal gains; the idea that if you break down everything you could think of that goes into riding a bike, and then improved it by 1 per cent, you will get a significant increase when you put it all back together.[1] Unfortunately, whilst Team GB cycling was focused on the marginal gains of performance improvement, their colleagues in Team Sky were losing sight of the marginal decays that can happen in integrity and honesty. Following a media furore over a 'jiffy bag' of unknown contents that was delivered to Sir Bradley Wiggins prior to a major cycling race, a 2018 report by UK MPs concluded that Team Sky had 'crossed an ethical line' because 'drugs were being used... to enhance the performance of riders and not just to treat medical needs'.[2] Losing integrity through small but daily acts of dishonesty is the opposite of Brailsford's mantra. Results may be delivered via the aggregation of marginal gains in performance but relationships and reputations are destroyed by the aggregation of marginal decays in integrity.

Sometimes this happens to an individual executive such as Sir David Brailsford; sometimes it happens to an entire organizational culture. As a researcher on trust, it is hard to shock me but reading the book *Bad Blood: Secrets and lies in a Silicon Valley startup* by John Carreyrou gave me a new benchmark regarding the extent to which a culture of dishonesty can take hold of, and destroy, an organization and its leaders.[3] The book is the story of the rise and fall of US biotech company Theranos, led by CEO Elizabeth Holmes. Over a 10-year period, Theranos raised more than $700 million from venture capitalists and private investors. At its peak in 2014, the company's value was $10 billion, with *Forbes* hailing Holmes as 'the youngest and wealthiest self-made billionaire in America'.[4] The Theranos board read like a 'Who's Who' of the good and great of America, including luminaries such as George Shultz (former US secretary of State), William Perry (former US Secretary of Defense), Henry Kissinger (former US Secretary of State) and Richard Kovacevich (former Wells Fargo Chairman and CEO). The company claimed to have invented a breakthrough blood-testing technology, but it turned out that the technology was fake.

Somehow, through Holmes' mesmeric and manipulative leadership, the company managed to keep this truth concealed for 10 years! Employees worked in a culture of fear and secrecy where anyone stepping out of line was immediately threatened via the country's most high-profile and intimidating lawyers. Eventually, under the scrutiny of *Wall Street Journal* investigator John Carreyrou, the lies were exposed and it all came down like a pack of cards. By 2019, the company had been declared bankrupt. Holmes' personal worth had dropped from $4.5 billion to zero, and the Securities & Exchange Commission (SEC) had charged both Holmes and the company president, Sunny Balwani, with 'massive fraud'. Their trial starts in August 2020, whilst the film of the book will be in a cinema near you shortly.

How does this happen? It happens through the aggregation of marginal decay: day by day, week by week, one conversation at a time. Dishonesty is like ivy: it creeps up on you. Turn your eye away for a moment and it takes root. It is easy to live with and yet, slowly but surely, it undermines the very fabric of an organization.

Furthermore, the red pill of transparency is changing the rules of the honesty game. In the past you could get away with the falsification of your CV, you could plagiarize other people's work or you could drop in the odd white lie because, to be blunt, it was most unlikely you would get found out. Now, we are all one click away from exposure. Everything about us is captured, catalogued and archived. There is nowhere to hide. The bar on honesty is rising. Yesterday's cheeky exaggeration is today's blatant lie. Yesterday's playful gamesmanship is today's headline cheat. How can we executive leaders possibly be the innocent white knights we are now expected to be?

The clue lies in the role that Miss Bell played for me when I was five years old. She asked the question: 'Has anyone seen Simon's Jonty West hat?' She held me accountable. On a different scale, it is the same role that John Carreyrou played for Theranos. They are asking the difficult questions. They are holding the company to account. It is the same role that the authorities played when stripping Lance Armstrong of his seven Tour de France victories. Asked questions and held to account. As Robert Louis Stevenson said, 'Sooner or later we all sit down to a banquet of consequences'. We are all tempted to be dishonest, particularly if we are ambitious and competitive, so who is asking you those tough questions that hold you to account? The earlier they ask those questions, the less the damage will be. As one of the CEOs I interviewed put it, 'every town needs a sheriff'; who is the sheriff in your organization and who is the sheriff in your life as a whole?

My wife, Jane, is my sheriff. She asks me questions that make me squirm. I try to wriggle out of them, but I know when I have been caught. Likewise, I have an executive coach who is my sheriff. I have deliberately given her that role: 'I want you to keep me honest'. It's great in theory but, in practice

I hate it. At one coaching session, we were reviewing my LinkedIn profile. She said to me, 'I notice you refer to one of your clients here. Have you asked their permission to do that?' Ouch! 'No, I haven't,' I meekly replied, before asking, 'Do you think that I should?' 'What do you think?' she pressed on. Ouch, again! 'Yes, you're right. I'll do that first thing tomorrow.' 'Good,' she concluded, leaving me with my tail firmly between my legs. It was a salutary lesson in being held to account for the aggregation of marginal decays.

So, first, I challenge you to be honest about your temptation to be dishonest. Someone as competitive and as ambitious as you must also have the potential to exaggerate and 'play the game'. You have the potential to fall into the attitude summed up by one CEO I interviewed: 'Over the last 15 years... there has been a far greater emphasis on the personal drive to succeed and if that means you screw someone else up then tough!' You're the sort of person that needs a sheriff; it's just a question of whether you can be honest about that fact. Let's assume you can. The next step is to appoint your sheriff. It could be your company chairman, a non-executive director, an internal mentor, an executive coach or someone in your private life. What makes for a great sheriff is someone you respect implicitly, who knows enough about you and the situation to spot the aggregation of marginal decays when they happen, yet still has the independence and bravery to hold you to account when you need to be challenged. It goes without saying that you cannot be your own sheriff; that would be like the manager of your favourite sports team volunteering to be the referee for the next home game. Trust me, it doesn't work.

Once you have appointed your sheriff, I want you to give them permission to ask the following four questions every time you come across a moral dilemma involving honesty. The questions utilize a powerful coaching technique known as 'perceptual positions'.[5] As with such methods, 'perceptual positions' is a sophisticated phrase for an everyday phenomenon. In this case, perceptual positions are more commonly referred to as 'looking at things from a different perspective'. Here are the four questions:

- What would you be doing regarding this situation if your decision was featured on the front page of tomorrow's national newspapers?
- If you shared this situation with your mother/father/brother/sister, what do you think they would say to you?
- If your future grandchildren were discussing your role in this situation, what would make them proud of you?

- If you communicated this decision to your suppliers/customers/owners/ partners what is the most difficult question they could ask you?

In summary, choosing to be honest is, first, about being honest about our own imperfections, including our temptation to distort the truth. Once we have swallowed enough pride to face that fact, we can appoint the sheriffs that we need in our lives, in our teams and in our organizations. We then create cultures in which the role of the sheriff is acknowledged, respected and rewarded. These people, and the difficult questions they ask, protect us from the aggregation of marginal decays; they keep our integrity intact.

 Choosing to be open

In reviewing the habits of integrity, let us turn from choosing to be honest to choosing to be open. According to a 2014 survey of over 1,600 managers by the Institute of Leadership and Management, openness is by far the most critical driver of trust – see Figure 4.1.[6] This finding was backed up by various CEO comments in my own research:

'The first way to build trustworthiness is through open communication. Consistent, open communication builds a belief that you are being told everything you need to be told.'

'Having a healthy mutual respect between the leader and the top team is crucial [to trustworthiness]. The CEO needs to "give of themselves" to achieve this.'

'As a Chair going into a company, I get an instinct about the CEO. It's really important what my gut feeling says about their trustworthiness. I'm testing it out all the time. I'm watching how open they are.'

'I have a one-to-one with everyone in the team at least once a quarter. We have "stand ups" every Monday morning to talk about what we are working on. I try to be as open as possible.'

But what is the difference between being honest and being open? Isn't being open simply speaking the truth? I think the clue to answering these questions lies in the two quotes above that mention CEOs giving of themselves and sharing of themselves. Being open goes beyond being honest; it involves speaking the truth and then giving something more. Being open requires leaders to expose themselves and reveal some vulnerability. As Patrick Lencioni put it, choosing to be open involves 'getting naked'.[7] In the book of

FIGURE 4.1   Which behaviours and skills drive trust?

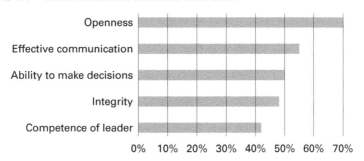

the same name, Lencioni writes: 'Vulnerability is integral to building powerful personal and business relationships, although it is often undervalued and misunderstood.' His notion goes against the grain of most leadership training, which has pigeon-holed vulnerability as a weakness. This is particularly the case with Western, male conditioning where men are conditioned from a young age to be strong. It also runs counter to the cultures of both military leadership and professional sport where we hail leadership role models for their ruthless invincibility.

We should note that while Lencioni regards choosing to be open as key to building powerful long-term relationships, it is not critical to winning a short-term victory. If all you want to do is win the battle or win the game, then there is no need to be open because it does not matter if your enemies do not trust you. For the same reason, if the sole focus of an executive leader's role is to maximize short-term profit, he or she does not need to be open. However, if you are tomorrow's executive leader and you are focused on delivering the triple bottom line as a trusted steward, then you will pride yourself on demonstrating trustworthiness with your stakeholders and you will choose to be open.

Another inspiring champion of vulnerability is Brene Brown. Brene captured her 12 years of research on the topic of vulnerability in her best-selling book *Daring Greatly*.[8] Bringing together a number of the habits of trustworthiness in one pithy quote, Brene Brown declares, 'Vulnerability sounds like truth and feels like courage. Truth and courage aren't always comfortable, but they're never weakness.' She then proceeds to discuss the 'armour' that we build to protect ourselves from vulnerability. We believe this armour keeps us safe but it numbs us to the reality of both the highs and the lows of business life. When we are numb we cannot empathize or relate to other people and, as executive leaders, this means we cannot engage their hearts as well as their minds. In the blue pill world this denial was tolerated, but the red pill of transparency exposes this approach as a limited coping mechanism. Armour shows up in many forms including excessive criticism of others, perfectionism and micro-management. These are all tactics to ensure others are 'found out' before we are. Yet, deep down, they mask insecurity. They mask the nagging realization that 'In the end, we are only tiny frightened animals, doing our best to survive amid other tiny frightened animals'.[9] I have coached enough leaders in business and in sport to know that their invincibility drops away quickly in a confidential, non-judgmental environment.

In my own career, I learnt a great deal about choosing to be open from the co-founders of Team 121, Rudi Bublitz and Iain Barker. Team 121 was one of the fastest-growing private companies in the UK in the period 1996–99. When I first joined this 70-person organization, I was shocked at the levels of openness shown by Rudi and Iain. For Rudi, it showed up in his dress sense: at one vitally important board-level sales pitch he wore an orange suit with polka-dot Dr Martin shoes! Incredibly, we won the work and afterwards when I asked the client why they had chosen us ahead of major players like Accenture and Deloitte Consulting, he replied, 'You were reassuringly amateurish.' I didn't know how to take his comment at the time, but now I realize that he was praising our vulnerability; Rudi's authentic dress sense was a symbol of the company's openness.

For Iain, his openness was more direct. I remember many a long flight with Iain where he would pour his heart out to me as we whiled away the time. I found it strangely inspiring. Here was this leader whom I greatly admired, who had built this fantastic company from nothing and yet he was not your typical bombproof hero. It was Leonard Cohen who sang that 'there's a crack in everything, that's how the light gets in' and, with Iain, you could see that his authentic vulnerability lit up the organization. What was supposed to be a weakness became a great strength. The company grew to 440 staff and, in 1999, I was proud to be part of the management board that sold the organization to Logica plc for £74.5 million.[10] Iain and Rudi became role models for many in that young company, including me. They had shown us a different and inspiring style of leadership, which had openness at its core.

So how do we put into practice the thinking of Lencioni and Brene Brown? Thankfully, they offer some tips in their work. Lencioni talks about the three fears that we need to overcome in order to be open: the fear of losing, of being embarrassed, and of feeling inferior. Lencioni's position is that if a client picks up that all you want to do is win, embarrass others with your invincibility and establish a position of superiority, you are not genuinely interested in helping them achieve their goals. Logically, they will then choose to work with an alternative supplier. What goes for clients also goes for other stakeholders. Being invincible is deeply unattractive if the other party has a choice and, in a red pill world, we all have a choice. However, note that Lencioni is not saying that we must always lose, get embarrassed and be inferior; he is saying that we must overcome the fear of those outcomes. The key to overcoming these fears is to reframe the situation.

Reframing is a powerful coaching technique. According to psychologist Paul Watzlawick and his team, 'To reframe means to change the conceptual setting in which a situation is experienced and to place it in another frame which fits the facts of the same situation equally well and thereby changes its entire meaning'.[11] You will all have had the experience of putting a photo into a new frame only to find it suddenly looked completely different. That is reframing. When it comes to our thoughts, we are always putting a frame around our thoughts and it is that frame that gives our thoughts meaning. The frame of reference we use for our thoughts consists of our beliefs and assumptions about a situation. So when we think to ourselves, 'I'm worried about losing or being embarrassed or feeling inferior' we are making assumptions about our objectives, our values and our worth. However, if we change our underlying assumption and beliefs we reframe the situation and the fear disappears. As soon as the fear disappears we become more confident and then, ironically, we are more likely to win.

In this book we have been busy reframing. We have reframed the purpose of business from the single bottom line to the triple bottom line of results, relationships and reputation. We have reframed the role of the executive leader from untrustworthy agent to trusted steward. This has created a different context in which to assess executive leadership behaviour. In this new frame, what we previously regarded as a weakness, ie vulnerability, has suddenly become a strength. So what is the reframe you need to make to ensure your company wins the war even if it involves losing a battle or two along the way? How, as a trusted executive, can you role-model that behaviour by giving of yourself and showing vulnerability in order to inspire trust? What deep assumptions do you hold about showing vulnerability that need to be re-examined if you are to step up, inspire your stakeholders and reach for a bigger game?

Choosing to be humble

There is an old Italian proverb that says, 'At the end of the game the king and the pawn go back into the same box.' I think this captures the essence of being humble; before we were executive leaders we were human beings and, after we have stepped down from those roles, we will be human beings again. Like choosing to be open, choosing to be humble runs counter to traditional leadership thinking. Stereotypical leaders are chest-beating alpha males who take every opportunity to self-promote and regard others as from an inferior gene pool. It was Jim Collins' book, *From Good to Great*[12] that first burst this myth in the popular psyche.

Based on a five-year research project, Collins concluded that the most effective leaders have a paradoxical combination of what he termed 'intense professional will and extreme personal humility'. These leaders were able to transform companies from good to great where 'great' involved outperforming the US stock market by an average 6.9 times over 15 years. Of the 1,435 companies that appeared on the Fortune 500 in the period 1965 to 1995 only 11 achieved this outcome. To illustrate his point, Collins cited the leader of Kimberley-Clark, Darwin Smith, who was CEO of the company for 20 years. In this period, Smith transformed Kimberley-Clark into the world's leading consumer paper products company, generating shareholder returns of 4.1 times those of the general market. Collins describes Smith in the following way:

> Compared with those [high profile] CEOs, Darwin Smith seems to have come from Mars. Shy, unpretentious, even awkward, Smith shunned attention. When a journalist asked him to describe his management style, Smith just stared back at the scribe from the other side of his thick black-rimmed glasses... Finally, after a long and uncomfortable silence, he said, 'Eccentric'. Needless to say, the *Wall Street Journal* did not publish a splashy feature on Darwin Smith.[13]

Collins called choosing to be humble 'Level 5 leadership'. The most impactful conclusion of his research was that, while Level 5 leadership is not the only factor, it is an essential factor if a company is to transform from good to great. In his own words, 'Good-to-great transformations don't happen without Level 5 leaders at the helm. They just don't'.[14] What makes this statement so powerful is that it is derived from empirical research, not from ideological musings. In other words, we might like to think that humble leaders are the most effective, but that is very different from proving this to be the case through rigorous scientific analysis.

CASE STUDY
Uber

Swaying to the music in the back of a taxi, Travis Kalanick, former CEO of Uber, would have had little idea that his career was about to take a dramatic turn.[15] On that night, Super Bowl Sunday 2017, Kalanick was being driven by one of his own Uber drivers, Fawzi Kamel, and at the end of the journey, a row erupted between the two of them. 'I'm bankrupt because of you,' said Fawzi, citing Uber's reduction in driver rates. After a round of verbal jousting, Kalanick lost his temper and berated Fawzi repeatedly calling his argument 'bullshit'. He then closed the conversation abruptly by saying, 'You know, some people don't like to take responsibility for their own shit'. With that, he got out of the cab and thought it was all done and dusted.

Unfortunately for Kalanick, a webcam in the taxi captured the whole conversation and the subsequent video went viral on social media. In this transparent, red pill world, Kalanick's lack of humility was broadcast around the world. The next day he was forced to issue an all-staff memo in which he apologized and stated that he 'must fundamentally change and grow up'. The apology came too late, as later that year Kalanick was forced to resign from his post by the investors due to various reputational misdemeanours. New Uber CEO, Dara Khosrowshahi, then issued his own all-staff memo in which he declared a new triple bottom line vision to change Uber from being 'a great product to being a great company that meaningfully contributes to society beyond the bottom line'.

I have shown the Travis Kalanick taxi video in many Trusted Executive Foundation workshops and afterwards I ask the audience to name which trust pillar and which trust habit they think led to the abrupt downfall of this highly successful CEO. Always people highlight that they see a lack of benevolence in Kalanick's behaviour. They describe him as 'rude' and 'arrogant'. It is this arrogance, or lack of humility, that most sticks in people's craw. Habit No.6, choosing to be humble, turned out to be the Achilles heel for this CEO.

Collins created a hierarchy of leadership in which each level accumulates skills that ultimately leads to the Level 5 capability – see Figure 4.2. In commenting on the difference between Level 4 and Level 5 leaders, Collins concluded that Level 4 leaders can sometimes generate short-term financial

FIGURE 4.2   Hierarchy of leadership

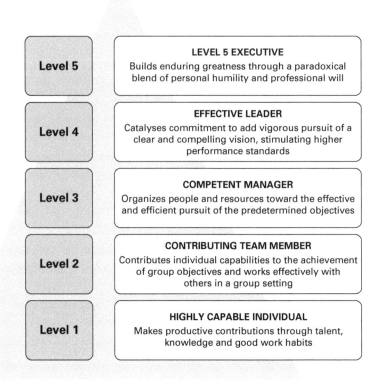

success through the power of their personal egos yet they struggle to sustain this success over the longer term. Furthermore, Level 4 leaders struggle to hand over successfully when they step down from the CEO role because they create a dependency on their own talents and confidence. The transition from Level 4 to Level 5 is about choosing to be humble and Collins describes four attributes that evidence that choice:

- Demonstrating a compelling modesty, shunning public adulation and never being boastful.
- Acting with quiet, calm determination and motivating others through inspired standards, not inspiring charisma.
- Channelling ambition into the company, not the self, and so setting up successors for even more greatness in the next generation.

- Looking in the mirror, not out of the window, when apportioning responsibility for poor performance.

Where do we look for our role models in Level 5 leadership? By definition, we are unlikely to find these leaders amongst the celebrity business figures we watch on TV or read about in the media. We are more likely to come across them at a personal level as we pursue our own careers. The CEOs I interviewed shared with me stories of Level 5 leaders who had influenced them at critical points in their own leadership development. Whenever they did this, their tone of voice changed and they spoke with some reverence about the humility they had witnessed. The following words from one interview are typical of the sentiment they expressed:

> I worked for a Permanent Secretary when I first went to Revenue & Customs who fell on his sword as a result of the scandal when tax-payers' data was lost. It was nothing to do with him and I found it emotionally very moving that he should stand down. He was a man of intense integrity. Your belief in the system is bolstered by somebody doing that and you think, 'Crikey, I'd rather some other people fell on their swords as well.'

In other interviews, I saw further glimpses of Level 5 leadership at work:

> 'To be a CEO you have to have a high degree of self-confidence but you're never fully in charge. It's not black and white. It's a balance of probabilities. You can skew these in your favour but you can't always be right, you can't always have the answer.'

> 'We have a tendency to say that if we do better than the average then it is down to our skill and if we do worse than the average then it is down to bad luck That attitude doesn't do anyone any good.'

> 'A lot of the great leaders in my working career are not extroverts, they don't shout and scream. People can achieve an awful lot without shouting and screaming about it.'

But if you are the Level 3 or level 4 executive leader of today how do you prepare yourself to be the Level 5 trusted executive of tomorrow? Collins did not research this question, though his own gut feeling was that some leaders have the Level 5 'seed' within them and others don't. My own hypothesis is that we all have the Level 5 'seed' within us, it is just that in some of us it is buried deeper than in others. Where I agree with Collins is that the qualities that get a leader to Level 4 (personal ambition, drive, confidence) are the same qualities that need to be transformed to reach Level 5. Marshall Goldsmith captured this irony in the title of his book, *What Got You Here, Won't Get You There*.[16]

Maybe the clue to this transition lies in Collins' use of the 'seed' analogy? What does it take for a once-dormant seed to sprout into life? We know the answer to this question.

Seeds grow when they experience the right conditions in their environment. When there is sufficient warmth, light and moisture they germinate and grow. When these conditions are not present the dormant seed will eventually die. Encouragingly, it can take a long time for a seed to die. Seeds of the Arctic lupin have been found in the burrows of Alaskan lemmings that date back to the end of the last ice age.[17] This should give us cause for hope!

What is the equivalent of warmth, light and moisture in the environment of a Level 4 executive leader? For me, it comes down to the leaders you surround yourself with: you are the company you keep. The leaders in your professional and personal network are either role-modelling the warmth, light and moisture of Level 5 leadership or they are role-modelling something colder, darker and dryer. Either way, you will be influenced by their presence. The American entrepreneur and speaker, Jim Rohn, took this principle to an extreme when he said, 'You are the average of the five people you spend the most time with'.[18] He went as far as to suggest that if you want to work out how much income someone earns all you need to do is to work out the average income of their five closest friends.

It's a scary concept even if it is only 50 per cent true. So what has science to say on this matter? American psychologist Professor Lawrence Rosenblum concluded that 'humans are incessant imitators'.[19] He researched how people subconsciously imitate the speech patterns of those around them, commenting that 'Sometimes we even take on the foreign accent of the person to whom we are talking, leading to embarrassing consequences.' Having worked internationally for many years I know exactly what he means; I have often found myself talking English in French, Dutch and German accents in various management meetings.

YOU ARE THE COMPANY YOU KEEP

Taking Rohn's assertion and Rosenblum's research and applying these to Level 5 leadership, it should prompt us to ask ourselves the following questions:

- Who are the five leaders in my personal and professional life I currently spend the most time with?
- Do these leaders exhibit the characteristics of Level 5 leadership in terms of choosing to be humble?
- How can I spend less time with those leaders who do not choose to be humble?
- Who are the five leaders I regard as the most humble in my wider personal and professional network?
- How can I spend more time with these people?
- What is the first step I am going to take to effect this change?

I personally experienced the power of this approach in my own career when I became a Board Chair for an organization called Vistage – the world's largest CEO membership organization. Vistage has upwards of 1,000 Chairs who mentor their member CEOs in peer groups of 12–16 with each group known as a private advisory board. Vistage attracted me to the Chair role through its strapline: 'from a life of success to a life of significance'. I now realize that this phrase sums up a Level 4 to Level 5 transition whereby you exchange the personal glory of Level 4 leadership for the understated yet more sustainable trusted stewardship of Level 5 leadership. When I attended my first Vistage Chair conference in New Orleans I realized I was standing in a room with 500 fellow Chairs who were all practising trusted stewardship. Many of these Chairs had been leading their Boards for 10, 20 and even 30 years! It was a unique and intimidating experience. Being in the company of those Chairs immediately humbled me. I knew that, as I mingled with that inspiring tribe, the experience was subtly rewiring my brain. I could feel myself stepping into their shoes: you are the company you keep.

DO HB CHECK SELF-ASSESSMENT

In this chapter we have covered the three habits of the pillar of integrity: choosing to be honest, to be open and to be humble. We have explored each of these habits through relevant coaching models, personal anecdotes and case studies. To embed this thinking further, it is time to revisit our mnemonic for the nine leadership habits that inspire results, relationships and reputation – DO HB CHECK:

D – deliver
O – open

H – humble
B – brave

C – coach
H – honesty
E – evangelize
C – consistency
K – kindness

Table 4.1 lists three behaviours under each of the three habits of integrity. Please take a moment to self-assess yourself against each of these behaviours. If you are working through this book with colleagues, you can also gain their perspectives on your behaviour and use these perceptions to establish your strengths and areas for development.

TABLE 4.1   DO HB CHECK self-assessment: habits of integrity

	Never	Rarely	Occasionally	Frequently	Always
I expect people to be scrupulously honest at work					
I demonstrate high standards of personal honesty					
I encourage honest and truthful workplace discussions					

TABLE 4.1 *continued*

	Never	Rarely	Occasionally	Frequently	Always

I am open to share personal thoughts and feelings when communicating with others at work

I praise others who show openness and vulnerability at work

I am willing to risk embarrassment by being open with others

When things go well I am willing to let others take the praise

When things go badly I am willing to take personal responsibility

Others would describe me as a very humble person

CEO coaching session – habits of integrity

It is time to see how an executive coach might work with a CEO to develop the habits of integrity. Compared to the habits of ability in the previous chapter, issues of integrity can be highly charged and sensitive. The following example coaching session highlights that difference through tackling an urgent, career-threatening situation. The coachee, Sue, is the CEO of a high-profile consumer goods company. Sue has only been in the post for six months and was previously the Director of Operations. Sue has engaged a coach to help her make a successful transition to the new role. Unfortunately, she has hit a crisis point and she has scheduled a coaching call at short notice to discuss this. While this dialogue is informed by my experience of working with CEOs, it is not based on any real person or actual event.

Coach: Good morning, Sue? What's the issue?

Sue: It never rains but it pours! When we finished our last coaching session a month ago I thought that all was progressing well. We'd completed a difficult round of redundancies, appointed a new Director of Finance and reorganized the marketing function. I went on holiday hoping that we had everything in order, then, halfway through my vacation, I get an e-mail from my Chair saying that he wanted to speak to me urgently.

Coach: Oh dear – not a good sign!

Sue: You can say that again. It turns out that one of the employees we made redundant had taken to Twitter to accuse the company of falsifying its accounts. To compound the matter, our Director of Communications was then contacted by a tabloid journalist and, under pressure, let out that we had recently appointed a new Director of Finance. The journalist put two and two together and writes an article suggesting that the previous Director of Finance was sacked for fiddling the books. All the while this was happening, I was sipping cocktails on the beach in Croatia.

Coach: ... then the Chair called.

Sue: Yes, and he's ranting and raving at me down the phone; asking me how much I knew and why I hadn't raised these topics earlier. Virtually accusing me of lying and then drops in that he wants me back on the next plane ready for a press conference tomorrow morning. That's when I got in touch with you to bring forward our coaching session, so that I can prepare for what is going to be an extremely gruelling exchange.

Coach: So what is the truth of the situation, Sue?

Sue: The truth is that there have been some poor accounting policies for which the previous Director of Finance was responsible. That is why we agreed a severance package for him. We tried to keep this confidential within the board, but these days it seems the walls have ears and the story must have got out.

Coach: 'Poor accounting policies'? What does that mean exactly?

Sue: For some years it had been custom and practice for the company to use some 'off-balance-sheet' vehicles to boost the perception of our profitability and financial stability as a business. I discovered this when I came in as CEO six months ago and decided that we needed to take action. However, rather than sacking the previous Director of Finance, I chose to take a more 'softly, softly' approach, because I was worried about the negative PR.

Coach: Sue, you know my thinking on these topics. This conversation strikes at the heart of your trustworthiness and the trustworthiness of your organization. On the one hand, I congratulate you on taking action to stop the dishonest accounting practice, but, on the other, I have to hold you to account for, first, trying to use your authority to control the truth and, secondly, for underestimating the drive for transparency that exists in your broader stakeholder groups, ie your employees and the press. Still, that is as it is. Our job now is to focus upon the future. How do you want to show up at the press conference tomorrow?

Sue: I've been thinking about this in relation to what you call the three habits of integrity. First, I think I was honest to stop the 'aggregation of marginal decay' in the accounting function by changing the Director of Finance. I have played the role of sheriff in that town. Unfortunately, I realize that where I went wrong was in not being sufficiently open about the issue with the rest of my stakeholders. I protected the reputation of the previous Director of Finance, but in the process I compromised my own integrity. I guess that in tomorrow's press conference I have the opportunity to correct that mistake by showing some vulnerability and being humble to take my share of responsibility for the situation.

Coach: That's a great summary. I think you played the sheriff role for the accounting function, but, unfortunately, no one was able to play that same role for you, since you were not sufficiently open about the challenge you were facing. You can't be your own sheriff and now you will need to face one or more of the fears that Lencioni talks about: the fear of losing, the fear of embarrassment or the fear of being inferior. If you show that level of vulnerability in the press conference tomorrow, I think there is still an opportunity to recover your trustworthiness. So let me ask you a question: how would one of Jim Collins' Level 4 leaders be handling the situation?

Sue: I guess a Level 4 leader would tough it out and continue to justify their actions. They would cling on to their position at any cost and they would be looking for an appropriate scapegoat to blame for the situation. On the other hand, a Level 5 leader would be taking the hit at a personal level and doing everything they could to protect the future reputation of the company. They would not give up the fight, but they would show 'personal humility' in accepting the personal consequences, for better or for worse.

Coach: And what is the worst personal consequence of this situation?

Sue: I could lose my job.

Coach: Yes, and that would feel like a crushing blow; an embarrassing and shameful personal defeat. What is the reframe that you could make to view that outcome as losing the battle and yet still winning the war?

Sue: That's a difficult question. I have dreamt of doing this job all my career. I believe I'm the best person to implement the changes the company needs to make and, in this situation, I think I did a lot of things right. Everyone makes mistakes, so why should I have to be the one who pays the price?

Coach: It sounds like you're saying it's not fair. How about the staff who you have recently made redundant? They lost their jobs. Do you think they felt that was fair?

Sue: We had to do that in order to protect the financial viability of the business. It was not their fault personally, but my job was to protect the wider whole.

Coach: So, if I was your Chair, I might say that this situation is similar. It is not totally your fault, but the wellbeing of the company is more important than the job of any one person. Recovering the trustworthiness of the company might only be possible under the direction of a new CEO. Let's go back to the reframe. What is the bigger picture view that means losing your job is a 'win/win' for both you and the company in the longer term?

Sue: If I fight to cling onto my job, my reputation will be damaged both in the current role and in any future CEO role I might have. Also, it will be harder for me to be successful in making the changes I need to make and I will be 'damaged goods' in the eyes of the market. I might struggle on for a further 12 months, but then fail spectacularly and effectively bring to an end my executive career. On the other hand, if I offer to resign then I recover my personal integrity. I may well be out of a job for some time, but I have the financial resources to cope with that. What's more, I think that if I resign, others will understand the predicament I have been in and will be more likely to view what happened as an isolated mistake they can forgive, rather than a permanent blemish on my character. Of course, it's still not a pleasant prospect, but I'm beginning to see a different picture.

Coach: It's not an easy situation, Sue. If I could think of an easier way out, I'd put it on the table. All I know is that you have a huge amount to offer in the CEO role and there are many others in your situation who have done the right thing and found that, in the long run, recovering their personal trustworthiness was worth far more than their immediate job title.

Sue: I need to think about this some more. It's a big decision. I'm still not sure what I am going to do, but you have given me a lot to think about. Thanks for the call. Let's speak again after the press conference tomorrow.

In the above session, Sue worked on all three of the habits of integrity: choosing to be honest, choosing to be open and choosing to be humble. On the one hand, she excelled at choosing to be honest in tackling an issue of integrity in the accounting function. Unfortunately, she fell short, in the eyes of some stakeholders, with regards to being open. She now faces a dilemma: whether to fight for her job or resign from the role. The coach used the work of Jim Collins on Level 5 leadership and the work of Patrick Lencioni on vulnerability to explore that dilemma in more detail. While it was tempting for the coach to ask Sue to make a decision there and then in the coaching session, she clearly needed to take some time to further think through the situation before coming to a final decision.

Endnotes

1   Hall, D, James, D and Marsden, N (2012) Marginal gains: Olympic lessons in high performance for organizations, *HR Bulletin: Research and Practice*, 7 (2), pp 9–13

2   Kelner, M (2018) Bradley Wiggins and Team Sky accused in damning drugs report, *Guardian*, https://www.theguardian.com/sport/2018/mar/05/bradley-wiggins-and-team-sky-accused-drugs-in-damning-report (archived at https://perma.cc/226P-M8GP)

3   Carreyrou, J (2019) *Bad Blood: Secrets and lies in a Silicon Valley startup*, Picador

4   Herper, M (2016) From $4.5 billion to nothing: Forbes revises net worth of Theranos founder Elizabeth Holmes, *Forbes*, https://www.forbes.com/sites/

matthewherper/2016/06/01/from-4-5-billion-to-nothing-forbes-revises-estimated-net-worth-of-theranos-founder-elizabeth-holmes/ (archived at https://perma.cc/Z22Z-QM6V)

5 Andreas, C and Andreas, T (2009) Aligning perceptual positions: a new distinction in NLP, *Journal of Consciousness Studies*, **16** (10–12), pp 217–30

6 Institute of Management and Leadership (2014) The truth about trust: honesty and integrity at work, https://www.institutelm.com/asset/1FECABB0-B108-4BE0-AA6DF8BA706F1831/ (archived at https://perma.cc/VT2T-DZTU)

7 Lencioni, P M (2009) *Getting Naked: A Business fable about shedding the three fears that sabotage client loyalty*, Vol 33, Wiley, Chichester

8 Brown, B (2012) *Daring Greatly: How the courage to be vulnerable transforms the way we live, love, parent, and lead*, Penguin, Harmondsworth

9 Hollis, J (2009) *What Matters Most: Living a more considered life*, Penguin, Harmondsworth

10 Barrie, C (1999) Logic dictates £50 m Logica signing, *Guardian*, 24 June

11 Watzlawick, P, Weakland, J H and Fisch, R (1974) *Change: Principles of problem formation and problem resolution*, W W Norton, London

12 Collins, J C (2001) *Good to Great: Why some companies make the leap – and others don't*, Random House, New York

13 Collins, J (2001) Level 5 leadership: The triumph of humility and fierce resolve, *Harvard Business Review*, **79** (1), pp 67–76

14 Ibid

15 Santora, J C (2020) *Dara Khosrowshahi: Changing the company culture at Uber*, Sage Publications

16 Goldsmith, M (2010) *What Got You Here Won't Get You There: How successful people become even more successful*, Profile Books, London

17 Burnside, O C *et al* (1996) Seed longevity of 41 weed species buried 17 years in eastern and western Nebraska, *Weed Science*, **44** (1), pp 74–86

18 Sandell, S (2015) You are the average of the five people you spend the most time with. Can this be true? *Huffington Post*, 21 October

19 Hough, A (2010) Humans 'subconsciously mimic other accents', psychologists claim, *Daily Telegraph*, 7 August

05

Pillar 3: Habits of benevolence

 Choosing to evangelize

'Evangelize' is an interesting word. It means to 'talk about how good you think something is'.[1] Some of us will be familiar with the word 'evangelize' in a religious context where spreading the good news involves creating new believers. My argument in this section is that the world of business desperately needs to create some new believers and, for this to happen, trusted executives will need to be more evangelical in their stakeholder communication. The reason for this is that bad news always did travel fast and now, because of digital transparency, bad news travels at the speed of light. As Guy Kawasaki stresses in *Harvard Business Review*, 'In the social age, evangelism is everyone's job.'[2] It's every executive leader's job because many people are talking each day about how bad your business is, not how good it is. We might call such people cynics. But whatever we call them, the harsh truth is that, no matter what your ability and your integrity, if you are not evangelizing then your trustworthiness will have a half-life; it will endure a daily decay.

Executive leaders are in the media spotlight. Some are celebrities jostling for position on the worldwide stage, shoulder to shoulder with the stars of sport, film and music. The rewards are high and with that comes an expectation that business leaders are public property. Every aspect of a CEO's professional and personal life is open to scrutiny by a merciless media – not just the traditional press, but also the endless recycling of views and opinions via social media. Here are some comments on this theme from the CEOs I interviewed:

'The media doesn't help this in lots of ways because they always want to pick out the piece that is going wrong without being held to account themselves.'

'[As CEO], you're the first port of call. You're the first point of failure. The moment you're above the radar with that failure, you're "dead meat".'

'If I say an inopportune thing, like Tony Hayward [ex-CEO, BP] did, then it's over so you're always on your guard.'

'If I am at a social event and the photographer wants to take a snap of a group saying "cheers" I won't be there. Because I know that if there is an incident in my organization then it will be that photograph, not a more serious one, that will be used by the press. And it could bring the organization down.'

'Trustworthiness isn't newsworthy. No one is going to put out a headline "CEO honours her promise". It's not a story, is it?'

As you read these comments, you may think these executive leaders feel sorry for themselves. We can paint ourselves as the victims in an ongoing drama with the media. Yet no one else regards us as victims. How could they when we earn what we earn, fly business class and attend the latest high-profile hospitality events? Is it really plausible that we can build our trust-worthiness by asking for sympathy from our stakeholders? Of course not. When bad news travels at the speed of light, the only effective response is to ensure that good news is travelling even faster. That is why I use the word 'evangelize' rather than 'communication', 'marketing' or 'branding'. That is why I regard choosing to evangelize as primarily a habit of benevolence not a habit of ability; it is an issue of personal passion not corporate function. Again, Kawasaki captures it well when he says, 'When you become an effective evangelist, you don't just promote your organization – you set an example for other employees.'[3] Evangelical executive leaders do not delegate this task to a specialist function or outsource it to a brand agency: they take personal ownership and build evangelical behaviour into their daily lives.

Not surprisingly, it is in the world's religions that we see the greatest examples of evangelism. The birth of a new religion reveals to us many of the characteristics of a successful evangelical approach. In the same way that today's executive leaders feel persecuted by the media, early religious evangelists were often persecuted, with many paying a heavier price than simply losing their business reputation. How did those early believers manage to spread their visions throughout the ancient world? Examining the relevant religious texts reveals some of their magic ingredients:

- A fervent, unshakeable belief in an inspiring vision.

- An ability to make the vision relevant to the immediate context.

- The emotional resilience to bounce back quickly from the darkest of days.

Let us look at one example: Paul of Tarsus. Paul set out for Rome seeking another opportunity to spread the good news of his own religious beliefs. A hurricane hit his ship off the coast of Crete. After many days of being battered by the storm the crew gave up hope of being saved. But Paul stood up and proclaimed, 'Keep up your courage for there will be no loss of life among you.' Sure enough, two weeks later the boat is shipwrecked at Malta, but with no loss of life. Paul puts his plans to get to Rome on hold and decides to preach to the Maltese islanders instead. Thus, Paul sets an early example of emotional resilience and a profound ability to bounce back from the bleakest of events and circumstances.

Compared to the world of executive leadership, I have experienced more noble visions and greater emotional resilience in the world of elite sport. Why is this? I can only conclude that sports athletes and coaches are clearer about why they do what they do. As an executive coach, I have had the privilege of working with Team GB sports coaches, England cricket and Premiership football clubs. What I have noticed about sports leaders and their athletes is that they love what they do and they have a dream. The dream may be to win an Olympic medal, or to walk out in front of 100,000 spectators at Melbourne Cricket Ground (MCG), or to lift the Cup but, whatever it is, the dream is exciting, risky and bold. Do you love being an executive leader? Do you know what your 'Olympic medal' looks like? Is it exciting, risky and bold?

Simon Sinek examines this issue in his book *Start with Why*.[4] According to Sinek, if you are driven by what you do and how you do it, you will attract people who want what you have. You will create one-off consumers who have no emotional attachment to your organization. However, if you are driven by *why* you do what you do, you will attract people who believe what you believe. You will create new believers and it is believers who will spread the good news about your products and services. It is believers who evangelize. He sums up his thinking in the 'golden circle' – see Figure 5.1. If you start at the centre of the circle and focus on the 'why', you will evangelize others with the clarity and power of your vision. Your 'why' creates your vision and this informs the triple bottom line goals of results, relationships

FIGURE 5.1   The golden circle

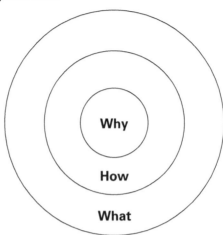

and reputation that we discussed in Chapter 2. As argued in that chapter, the first challenge for executive leaders is to work at the level of purpose, not solely at the level of profit. The habit of choosing to evangelize reminds us of the reason for that starting point.

However, in my experience, the world of elite sport can learn from the world of business when it comes to the third aspect of choosing to evangelize: making the vision relevant to the immediate context. Not everyone is cut out to be an Olympian or an England cricket captain. Most of us are mere mortals who are swept up and down by the vagaries of our working lives. Some days we feel like packing it all in. Some days we just can't put on a brave face, we rail against the world and we bemoan our bad luck. On those days, the 'bullet-proof', uber-optimistic CEO is an alien being to whom we cannot relate; someone who does not inspire us, but who frightens us with his or her relentless positivity. So when we are engaging our future believers we need to first empathize with their current experience of reality. Through empathy we build trust and through trust we open the door to influence.

To build that empathy, we must first get alongside and pace others before we can lead them; when they 'zig' we need to 'zig', when they 'zag' we need to 'zag'. Executive leaders are adept at engaging a variety of stakeholders including owners, customers, staff, media and pressure groups. Often they operate across international boundaries and this gives them a valuable cosmopolitan outlook that I have encountered less often in the sporting coach or athlete. All of our stakeholders have an agenda. Our job is to understand that agenda, relate to it and give it some time before pressing on with our own vision. As the old saying goes, 'You can't really understand another person's experience until you've walked a mile in their shoes.' You can't choose to evangelize until you've connected with the immediate world of your future believers.

CASE STUDY

Peter Moores: former Head Coach of the England cricket team

I started this section highlighting the role of the media in casting a cynical eye on the world of executive leadership. It is in the face of media scrutiny that our evangelical skills are tested to the limit. The greatest evangelist I have worked with is Peter Moores, coach of the England cricket team in the periods 2007–09 and 2014–15. During the cricket world cup of 2015, I was having weekly coaching calls with Peter as England suffered a humiliating early exit from the tournament. It never ceased to amaze me that Peter would bounce into each call bubbling with enthusiasm and positivity, despite the daily torrent of angst and derision that was poured on him by the national press. It was the same in his press conferences: constantly upbeat, focused on winning the next game and immune to the politics and negativity that surrounded him.

He was once accosted in a hotel bar by a correspondent of the tabloid press who, in utter frustration, cried out, 'But Peter you're always so positive!' To which he got the blunt reply, 'Well, thank God for that!' Peter was crystal clear about why he did what he did: he loved cricket. It was never about him and it was always about the good of the game. Once he commented to me, when discussing the constant threat of being sacked, 'You've got to remember, John, this job doesn't define who I am.' It wasn't a glib cliché. Peter 'walked the talk'. His mindset and attitude act as a benchmark for all trusted executives who step out on the evangelical path.

 Choosing to be brave

When I was a teenager, I was given a copy of the serenity prayer and, for some reason, it grabbed my attention.[5] It was written on a wooden plaque which I stuck on my bedroom mirror with a huge wad of Blu-Tac. With some irony, every morning when I looked at my acne-ridden features, I read the words:

God, grant me the serenity to accept the things I cannot change,

The courage to change the things I can,

And the wisdom to know the difference.

I still love those words and they capture the essence of why choosing to be brave is one of the nine leadership habits that inspire results, relationships and reputation. Try as I might as a teenager, I couldn't change the fact that I had acne. I had to learn to accept it. However, as an executive leader there are many things that you can change and choosing to be brave is often a prerequisite to 'sticking your neck out' for the greater good. We are not talking here about the traditional bravery of the heroic leader charging into battle on his white steed crying, 'Follow me!' We are talking about the more subtle bravery of the post-heroic leader who knows when to swallow hard and make a selfless act; an act of benevolence that protects others in the face of corporate tyranny. In this context, the bravery required for trustworthiness is not physical bravery or personal bravery but moral bravery. As one of my CEO interviewees calmly said, 'There are very few people who have the balls to walk into a corporate environment and risk their own situation to rock the boat.' Are you one of those chosen few?

Many of you will know the film *12 Angry Men* (directed by Sidney Lumet in 1957). It is the story of a jury that is tasked with judging the guilt of a young black man who is facing trial for murder. The jury members retire to consider the evidence, and they decide to conduct a preliminary vote. The foreman states, 'All those voting guilty, please raise your hands.' One by one, hands are raised and the foreman counts 11 guilty votes. 'Those voting not guilty?' he enquires and a solitary hand is raised. At this point, one of the other jurors sarcastically intervenes: 'Boy, oh boy, there's always one,' he bemoans. There's always one. Are you prepared to be the one who holds up your hand when everyone else is keeping quiet? Or will you go with the flow and hope that it's someone else's turn to be morally brave?

In the film, the lone objector calmly proceeds to convince the others on the jury that the defendant is innocent and there is a happy ending as the young man is acquitted. In real life, this does not always happen. Who, inside the system, was morally brave enough to put up their hand when the UK banks were rigging the inter-bank lending rate? No one. Who, inside the system, was morally brave enough to put up their hand when Lance Armstrong was corrupting the Tour de France with his systematic use of performance-enhancing drugs? No one. And, as a result, we lose trust in these systems. And even when someone lower down the tree demonstrates moral bravery, we stigmatize their behaviour with the label 'whistle-blower', pouring venom and scorn on their attempts to reveal the truth. As Ernest Hemingway commented, rare indeed are the leaders who rise above the 'group-think' of their fellow men:

> Few men are willing to brave the disapproval of their fellows, the censure of their colleagues, the wrath of their society. Moral courage is a rarer commodity than bravery in battle or great intelligence. Yet it is the one essential, vital quality of those who seek to change a world which yields most painfully to change.[6]

One of the most chastening experiences of my own corporate career involved an incident when I did not choose to be morally brave. One of my staff told me some information which incriminated another senior leader. I was told in confidence and I kept that confidence. Some months later, the senior leader involved had been sacked for gross misconduct and I found myself being grilled in front of the board by the Group Chief Operating Officer. 'Did you know about this situation, John?' he asked while staring me in the eye. 'Yes, I did,' I replied, 'but I was sworn to confidence.' As soon as the words left my lips I knew that I had made a mistake. I had kept the trust of one individual and yet lost the trust of the organization's leadership. It was a lesson I have never forgotten: the bravest call is the call that protects the integrity of the entire system rather than the integrity of any one individual or group within that system.

I hope it is now clear how choosing to be morally brave contributes to the pursuit of trustworthiness. Yet the more challenging question is, 'How do we develop such bravery?' How do we make sure we raise our hand and we speak up at the right time and in the right way? Isn't bravery something we are born with rather than a quality we develop? The words of Mark Twain help us look deeper into this challenge: 'Courage is resistance to fear, mastery of fear... not absence of fear.' In other words, it is necessary to be scared in order to be brave. Bravery is not being *fearless*; it is the capacity to act in the presence of fear. Some people are scared of spiders. We call this arachnophobia. Some people are scared of open spaces. We call this agoraphobia. The fear of being morally brave is the fear of social rejection; it is a phobia like all the others. However, this phobia is so common it doesn't even have a name and the nameless phobias are the most dangerous of all; their lack of identity tempts us into thinking they are just a fact of life. As soon as we realize that choosing to be morally brave involves overcoming a phobia, we have transformed it from something we passively accept to something we can change and overcome.

In my coaching work, I have witnessed three successful techniques for overcoming phobias:

- Creating a counter-emotion to fear that spurs action.

- Progressive exposure and desensitization to the fear.

- Visualization work to diminish the 'catastrophizing excesses' of the human mind.

When it comes to moral bravery the emotion that spurs action is often anger. In fact, according to positive psychology researcher, Robert Biswas-Diener, the only emotion that can overcome fear is anger.[7] He cites research by Lerner and Keltner,[8] which found that angry people are more likely to take risks, see themselves as in control and feel more positive about future outcomes. In my experience, anger is an underutilized emotion in organizational life. We tend to think of anger as the unpredictable boss who 'flies off the handle' at the slightest provocation. However, felt anger is different to expressed anger. Felt anger is a powerful antidote to the fear of social rejection. Expressed anger is likely to hurt others. If we get in touch with our sense of anger in a situation this can help us be morally brave. And here there is a link to the habit of choosing to be consistent and our earlier work on values; for in most situations where you are required to be morally brave, one of your core values is being trampled upon. As Biswas-Diener says, 'You can work yourself into a courageous mindset by focusing upon the ways in which your most precious values are being trampled.' To do this you first need to know what your values are.

The second technique for overcoming phobias is what psychologists call 'exposure therapy'[9] whilst the rest of the world refers to it as 'taking it one step at a time'. Research has shown that if you expose people to their fear trigger (for instance, spiders), in stages over time, their fears gradually diminish. Hence, when choosing to be morally brave it helps to practise this approach in situations that are less threatening than others. For example, it is easier to say, 'No, I disagree, that's rubbish' to your friend than it is to your boss. It is easier to 'draw the line' with your compliant seven-year-old child than it is with your rebellious teenager. It is typically easier to make a bold speech in front of 15 people than it is to do so in front of 500. But the real point is that if you don't start small today then you will never act big tomorrow. If you don't challenge your friend you will never challenge your boss. If you don't challenge your seven-year-old you will one day face a rebellious teenager. If you want to choose to be morally brave then, by all means, begin small but please begin now.

Finally, I have witnessed dramatic impacts in removing phobias using the visualization technique that experts refer to as the 'fast phobia cure'.[10] The fast phobia cure is a way of rewriting traumatic memories so that when a phobia trigger appears (spider) the brain does not start catastrophizing about the possible consequences ('it's a poisonous spider, it's going to bite you, you're going to scream and then you will die'). I liken the fast phobia cure to saving a Word document when the software helpfully comes back with the message 'You already have a file named "x". Do you want to replace it with this one?' When it comes to over-writing phobias the answer is always, 'Yes, I do, thanks'.

FAST PHOBIA CURE FOR MORAL BRAVERY

Here is a simple seven-step script for a fast phobia cure when the challenge is to overcome the social rejection we fear when being morally brave:

1　Think of a time when you experienced social rejection by speaking up to challenge the status quo. Remember that you were ok before and after the unpleasant experience.

2　Now imagine yourself sitting in an empty cinema watching a small, black-and-white screen.

3　Float out of the cinema seat and into the projection booth. You can now see yourself in the seat watching the film on the screen.

4　Run the film of the unpleasant memory on the screen in black and white. Make sure you run it from the beginning to the end.

5　Now run the film backwards quickly in full-colour. This should take only one or two seconds.

6　Repeat steps 4 and 5 and this time, when you run the film backwards, add a happy musical soundtrack to the film.

7　Finally, think again of the original memory and note your emotional response. How has it changed?

The fast phobia cure works by disassociating you from the original memory and giving you a more objective perspective on the situation. It drains the emotion from the scene and so re-empowers you to be bolder in your future behaviour. In many ways, this technique is similar to the 'reframing' approach discussed in Chapter 4; both techniques encourage a shift in perspective in order to release us from limiting beliefs, negative emotions and narrow thinking. The new mindset then protects us from a lapse in our trustworthiness. (For more information and examples of the use of these and similar techniques, I would recommend reading Lynne Cooper's jargon-free book, *Business NLP for Dummies*.[11])

In this section, we have recognized that the habit of choosing to be brave targets a specific sub-set of bravery: the idea of moral courage as distinct from physical and personal courage. The bravery that contributes to trustworthiness is choosing to speak up and make a stand for the wider good even when such acts risk social rejection. These are priceless acts of benevolence. Using the above techniques, we can 'feel the fear and do it anyway', as Susan Jeffers titled her best-selling book.[12] We treat social rejection as a phobia and then we use proven phobia cures to build our bravery over time.

CASE STUDY

John Spedan Lewis: founder of the John Lewis Partnership

There is no greater social rejection than to be cast off by your family, so let us end this section by reminding ourselves of an inspiring example from the corporate world of choosing to be morally brave. The UK retailer, John Lewis Partnership, is one of the most trusted brand names in the marketplace. Its first store opened in Oxford Street, London, in 1864 and it now has 43 stores and over 90,000 staff.

As part of my research, I interviewed Jane Tozer, a former non-executive director of John Lewis. Jane shared with me the inspiring story of John Spedan Lewis, son of the original founder, John Lewis. Spedan Lewis had bold ideas, including the radical notion of distributing the profits of the company to its staff. His father regarded him as a 'communist' and rejected him both professionally and personally. The company split, with John Lewis taking control of the original store in Oxford Street and Spedan Lewis having sole ownership of the second store, which was branded 'Peter Jones'. Spedan Lewis implemented his new working practices in the Peter Jones store, turning it round from a loss-making business to one that was highly profitable. Upon his father's death in 1928, Spedan Lewis signed the 'First Trust Settlement', enshrining the company's operating principles and laying the foundation for a sustained period of financial success based on a reputation for market-leading trustworthiness.

Executive leaders such as Spedan Lewis had no access to psychological theory; they didn't attend ethical leadership courses at Harvard Business School and they didn't engage executive coaches. They worked it out for themselves and then chose to do the right thing. Their pioneering example should rightly humble us.

 ## Choosing to be kind

Some years ago, I was sat in a meeting at the headquarters of Mondelez International, the global confectionery group. While the meeting was in mid-flow, the door opened and a lady walked in. She quietly placed a Mondelez branded bag next to my chair. Then she left. I was tempted to look in the bag, but I was worried about getting distracted from the meeting so I left it alone. But it kept nagging me and eventually I leant over, opened the bag and took a peek inside. The bag was full of chocolates. I assumed there had been a mistake and, at the end of the meeting, I raised it with the chairperson. 'Oh yes, they're for you,' she said. 'Every visitor that comes to this building gets a bag of chocolates. It fits with our value of creating random acts of kindness.' Free chocolates? For me? What was the catch? There didn't seem to be one. I drove home feeling like a child on Christmas Day morning. Rushing into the kitchen, I said to my wife and two sons, 'Look I've got some free chocolates.' They looked at me in dismay, wondering how a few chocolates could have made my day. But it wasn't the chocolates that had made my day; it was the random act of kindness. And somehow it had changed my attitude towards Mondelez International; I trusted them more.

A random act of kindness (RAK) is a selfless act intended to bring help, happiness or joy to another person. The phrase is sometimes credited to Anne Herbert, who wrote the words 'practice random acts of kindness and senseless acts of beauty' on a place mat at a Sausalito restaurant in 1982. RAK initiatives have since sprung up in many different guises, often catalysed by social media. Choosing to be kind is a well-established habit in some communities. The working classes of Naples have a tradition whereby any person who has experienced financial good fortune pays for two coffees at the local café, but receives and drinks only one. The second coffee is referred to as the 'caffé sospeso' and can be claimed for free by anyone who asks if a sospeso is available. Do you offer random acts of kindness in your corporate community? Do you have any free sospesos available for your stakeholders?

Choosing to be kind can be an isolated act that requires no further justification. However, since benevolence is one of the three pillars of trustworthiness, we can see that choosing to be kind is at the heart of the trust-building challenge. And choosing to be kind is important regardless of our prowess in the habits of ability and integrity. In a leadership context, this point is neatly illustrated in the film *The Imitation Game*, the true story about how a team of British code-breakers, led by the prodigy Alan Turing, broke the German Enigma code in World War II.[13] There was no doubting the ability of Turing; he was a genius with a first in mathematics from Cambridge University. Equally, there is no evidence that he was lacking in integrity. However, in the film, despite these qualities, Turing struggles to gain the trust of his team. In exasperation, he turns for advice to his confidante and friend Joan Clarke. Joan confronts Turing with the uncomfortable truth: 'Alan, [regardless of your brilliance], you're going to need all the help you can get and they are not going to help you if they don't like you.' Suitably humbled, Turing is later seen offering his bemused colleagues some free apples at one of their lunch breaks. It is his random act of kindness and, despite his awkwardness, the act represents the turning point in his relationship with the team. They already knew he was fantastically clever, they did not doubt his integrity and now they had glimpsed his kindness; in their eyes he had become a trusted steward.

Why is it that choosing to be kind is critical to trustworthiness? The psychological theory of transactional analysis (TA) sheds some light on this question. TA proposes that we are each made up of three psychological 'ego-states': a parent-state (P), an adult-state (A) and a child-state (C).[14] Each ego-state plays a particular role in our overall personality – see Figure 5.2. We can see that the parent-state is our 'taught' concept of life, the adult is our 'thought' concept of life and the child is our 'felt' concept of life. TA is typically used to help people explore how best to communicate with others. However, it can also shed light on the world of trustworthiness. We can see that, in the blue pill world, we were taught to trust authority figures. For example, when you were a child your parents may have said 'You should trust the prime minister' and you might have asked, 'Why?' and they replied, 'Because he is the prime minister that's why' (parent ego-state). In the absence of access to other information (adult ego-state) you trusted what they said. But when you grew up, you started to do your own research (adult ego-state) and you decided that some prime ministers could be trusted more than others. In this context, we can see that the red pill of transparency is the worldwide awakening of the adult ego-state; the collective access to

FIGURE 5.2   Ego-states

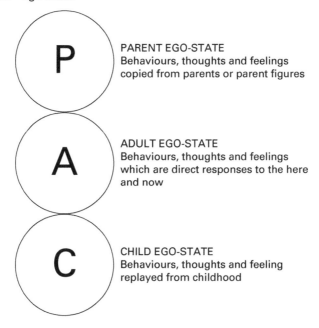

PARENT EGO-STATE
Behaviours, thoughts and feelings
copied from parents or parent figures

ADULT EGO-STATE
Behaviours, thoughts and feelings
which are direct responses to the here
and now

CHILD EGO-STATE
Behaviours, thoughts and feeling
replayed from childhood

massive repositories of open information via the internet. The crumbling of the pillar of authority is the collapse of the parent ego-state as a means of controlling others. Amidst this fundamental transformation the child can get very scared indeed! Why? Because traditionally the child sought protection from the parent and if the parent ego-state is weakened, where will the child find care and protection? It must now find it from within the adult ego-state when the adult chooses to be kind.

This dialogue between parent, adult and child ego-states goes on inside your organization, in your leadership team and in your own head. If we wish to become a trusted executive, we must recognize the needs of the child ego-state and choose to satisfy these needs in the here and now. If we fail to do this then, despite our abilities and our integrity, the child will still get scared and the child ego-state will say, 'I don't trust you.' Now, you could reply, 'Well, you should do because I am capable and honest,' but I hope you can see that this is a parent-state response to a child-state request and, trust me, it will not work. What works in satisfying the needs of the scared child is choosing to be kind, choosing to care and choosing to protect.

Choosing to be kind is not about big dreams such as finding a cure for cancer; it is about taking small steps on a daily basis, steps that touch the lives of the people around us. As the saying goes, 'You may have a heart of gold, but so does a boiled egg. We are remembered for our actions.' The good news is that the child ego-state notices little actions, not grand gestures. The child does not trust grand gestures; the child trusts regular, low-profile acts of kindness, acts which Webster refers to as TNTs (tiny noticeable things).[15] TNTs are like bonsai trees: they are miniature in scale yet perfectly formed. The value of TNTs is measured by the depth of thoughtfulness that has gone into their design. TNTs are transformative in leadership relationships because they operate outside the paradigm of profit that we examined in Chapter 2. Here are a few examples of TNTs that I have experienced:

- A handwritten 'thank you' note that a CEO gave to all the members of a small project team.
- A CEO turning up unannounced to a Sunday afternoon crisis meeting.
- An executive leader arriving home 30 minutes early with a bunch of flowers.
- A birthday card received from your employer signed by all the head office staff.

The best TNTs remain secrets. I could share them with you in this book, but you would not relate to them. They are so personal that they are meaningful only to the people present at the time. They are the equivalent of private jokes – the funniest jokes of all, yet the ones with the shortest and most limited lifespan. Therefore, the challenge for you is to design and implement your own TNTs. The good news is that your TNTs become more powerful as you become more senior in the organization. This is because the people around you assume you are the typical executive leader 'parent-state' stereotype; too busy to show them the personal touch. For this reason, I like to say to my CEO clients that the best thing about their jobs is that they can make someone's day every day: a sincere 'thank you', a precise 'well done', an unnecessary text to say 'happy birthday'. Pure gold dust. What a great job that is!

'Kindness' is not a word that has worked itself into the business lexicon yet, but it is coming sometime soon. We can predict this because the closely related words of 'care' and 'empathy' are suddenly in the mainstream of business life. Consider these quotes from the CEOs I interviewed:

> 'We have put all 600 staff through a week-long course in the skills of empathy. It's an expensive programme but we've done it so that we can convince the consumer that we care.'

'The CEO doesn't need to do everything but they do need to care about everything.'

'My three Cs are clarity, consistency and care.'

'A lack of care for the principal stakeholders destroys trustworthiness.'

'Every customer that complains gets a letter back from the CEO. Those customers go straight on social media and cry "Hallelujah! This company cares about me." And let's be honest, in this country that is quite unusual.'

I have spoken in this section a great deal about the power of choosing to be kind as a trust-building tool. I would like to close with a story about the equal and opposite power of how a lack of kindness destroys trust. In my mind, the opposite of kindness is not cruelty but negligence. Negligence is a lack of care; it is passive and it is dismissive. I experienced negligence early in my own career when escorting an important client from the meeting room to the lift in our company headquarters. As we approached the swing doors in the corridor, I noticed one of the managing directors (MDs) coming in the opposite direction. My client and the MD hit the door at the same time and got in a muddle. At this point, I heard the MD shout, 'Just get out of the f-ing way!' The moment passed and, embarrassed, I tried to hush over the incident as my client disappeared into the lift. We never did any further business with that client and that MD never knew why that was; but I did.

You never know when today's small gestures of kindness or casual negligent asides might be harvested by your future self. Managers manage. Leaders anticipate.

DO HB CHECK SELF-ASSESSMENT

In this chapter we have covered the three habits of the pillar of benevolence: choosing to evangelize, to be brave and to be kind. We have seen that, compared to the habits of ability and integrity, these are habits of the heart that lay the emotional foundation of trustworthiness. For the final time, we revisit our mnemonic for remembering the nine habits:

D – deliver

O – open

H – humble

B – brave

C – coach

H – honesty

E – evangelize

C – consistency

K – kindness

Listed in Table 5.1 are the habits of benevolence with three behaviours under each habit. Take a moment to self-assess yourself against each of these behaviours. If you are working through this book with colleagues, you can also gain their perspectives on your behaviour and use these perceptions to establish your strengths and areas for development.

TABLE 5.1   DO HB CHECK self-assessment: habits of benevolence

	Never	Rarely	Occasionally	Frequently	Always
At work, I promote a passionate and inspiring vision					
I am resilient to bounce back quickly from disappointments					
At work, it is clear to others that I love what I do					
I am brave to speak out for the wider good even at the expense of my own self-interest					
I have the courage to act against the status quo rather than compromise on my principles					
I praise others in my workplace who make a stand based on their principles and values					

TABLE 5.1 *continued*

	Never	Rarely	Occasionally	Frequently	Always
I practise random acts of kindness in the workplace					
I show empathy and care when dealing with others at work					
I expect others to show care and kindness at work					

As we complete our exploration of the Nine Habits that inspire results, relationships and reputation, it is time to take stock. You may be feeling overwhelmed with the scale of the challenge. How can I, or anyone else, become this ideal of trustworthiness? Well, as the Chinese philosopher, Lao Tzu, said, 'A journey of a thousand miles begins with a single step.' The first step in becoming a trusted executive is self-awareness. The fact that you have read this book up to this point will already have raised your awareness. If you have taken the time to complete the DO HB CHECK questionnaires at the end of each chapter this will have taken your self-awareness to the next level. (If you have been tempted to skip these questionnaires, as I often have done when reading similar books, I would encourage you to go back and do them now.)

Take a moment now to use Figure 5.3 to reflect on all Nine Habits of Trust.

As you look at the full range, ask yourself the following questions:

- What are your strongest trust-building habits?
- If there was one habit that you could focus upon that could make the most impact on your own leadership, which would it be?
- What are the strongest trust-building habits in your organizational culture?
- Which habit could most help your organization drive the triple bottom line of results, relationships and reputation?

FIGURE 5.3   The Nine Habits of Trust

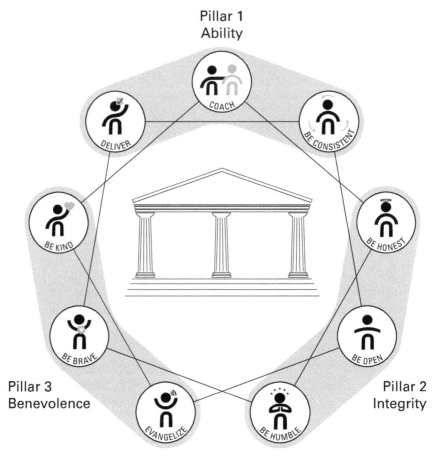

- What one habit could trip you up as a leader or a brand if you do not give it sufficient attention?
- What is one action that you could take to build the muscle of your chosen trust habit in the coming week?

To give you an example, my own core strengths would be choosing to deliver, choosing to coach and choosing to be brave. My habit that needs further development is Habit No. 5 – choosing to be open. As an alpha male leader, I was taught to not show weakness and this trait was role-modelled for me by various male authority figures in my career. My attitude towards vulnerability is best summed up by the Brene Brown quote, 'Vulnerability is the first thing I want to see in you and it is the last thing I want you to see in me.'[16] Somewhat late in life I am learning that as a leader I need to go first with vulnerability. At the right time and in the right place, I need to show some human fallibility. I need to bare a bit more of my soul in order to bring others closer into my circle of trust.

Armed with this knowledge, we can make decisions that play to our strengths and we can seek help for the areas of further development. Where can we find such help? Here are some options:

- Complete the exercises in this book for your chosen habits and follow up the relevant references at the end of each chapter.

- Work on your chosen habits with an executive coach or internal mentor.

- Work on your habits in a confidential leadership peer group such as those facilitated by the Trusted Executive Foundation (https://trustedexecutive. com/journey-of-trust/community/ (archived at https://perma.cc/HX8T-S3GS)) or other similar organizations.

- Get confidential feedback on your individual and organizational trust habits by using the 360 feedback tool or the online trust survey that have been developed by the team at the Trusted Executive Foundation (www. trustedexecutive.com).

I hope these tips allow you to take your own next step in becoming a leader, a team and an organization that inspires trust. But, however much progress you make, you will still make mistakes. Knowing how to recover quickly from these is the focus of our next chapter.

CEO coaching session – habits of benevolence

In this, our final example of a CEO coaching session, the coach will work to develop the habits of benevolence. The session will highlight how it is often counter-intuitive for an executive leader to regard kindness, moral bravery and evangelizing as resources that improve their effectiveness in the CEO role. Therefore, the coach has to be creative to trigger a mindset shift. In this coaching scenario, the coachee, Mark, is a board member of a private engineering company. Mark is part of a 'Journey of Trust' leadership development programme in which all the participants are assigned an executive coach and undertake a Nine Habits 360 feedback exercise at the start of the programme. In an earlier coaching session the Nine Habits feedback report has been debriefed and Mark is working on his development areas. While this dialogue is informed by my experience of working with CEOs, it is not based on any real person or actual event.

Coach: Mark, let's have a look at how you are getting on with this challenge of building high-trust relationships in the boardroom. Your 360-degree feedback report clearly highlighted this as a development area. What are your thoughts about it?

Mark: As you know, I'm very task-focused. Give me a plan, an objective and a deadline and you can count on me to get the job done, but sometimes there will be some 'collateral damage' in terms of people and relationships. I think that is one of my strengths and that is largely how I got to be promoted into this role. However, the issue now is that, as a board member, I see things that need doing in the organization, but I don't have the authority to make them happen on my own. I have to build coalitions and partnerships, both inside and outside the organization, and this is not my natural strength.

Coach: So you accept the feedback that this is an area for improvement?

Mark: Yes, I accept the feedback. I just don't know what to do about it. I keep coming up with a plan to build better relationships in the boardroom and then converting into tasks and deadlines, but then I realize that I am just reinforcing my previous task-centred habit. As someone told me recently, 'When the only tool you've got is a hammer, everything looks like a nail.'

Coach: I get it. You're facing a right-brain challenge of building relationships and trying to use a left-brain problem-solving approach to crack it. And you realize that is not going to work. I'd like to suggest an alternative approach. I'd like us to work with a metaphor to get the creative juices flowing. Are you up for that?

Mark: Yes. Sounds like fun. Go for it.

Coach: Some time ago, I was climbing the Eiffel Tower in Paris with my family. I guess we must have been three-quarters of the way up when I came across a young man who had frozen on the steps. He stood like a human statue poised to make his next step. But he couldn't make that next step, because he had just discovered that he was scared of heights. He'd come a long way, but he had hit a new problem that was preventing him going further. And that problem was an irrational fear of heights. Everyone was staring at him, silently urging him on, but he was paralyzed by fear. Now let's imagine you were with me in that moment and I asked you in your task-centred mode to go and solve that problem. What would you do?

Mark: Oh, that's easy. I'd march up to the guy and say, 'Come on. Pull yourself together. All you need to do is put one foot in front of the other, exactly as you have been doing up until now, and you'll be up the top of this tower in a flash.'

Coach: And what do you think the impact of that behaviour would be?

Mark: [laughs] I think I would just make him angry. I'd come over as arrogant, uncaring and lacking in any sort of inspiring vision. It would be totally ineffective.

Coach: Ok. What behaviour do you think would be more effective in that situation?

Mark: I'd have to empathize with the guy first. I'd have to show him that I care, so that he might trust me. Thinking of the habits of benevolence, I suppose I'd have to show kindness and, once I'd built some sort of relationship, I could then evangelize to him about the fantastic views from the top of the tower and this might motivate him to keep going, despite his fear of heights.

Coach: That's the theory. Let's try putting it into practice. Imagine you're walking up to the young man. What would you say to him if you were being kind and empathizing with him?

Mark: I imagine that...

Coach: No, I don't want you to imagine doing it. I want you to do it. What would you say?

Mark: [long silence] I don't know what I would say.

Coach: That's fine. Take some more time.

Mark: [long silence] Ok, here goes... 'Don't beat yourself up... There's a reason why you're feeling like this... These things happen... What can I do to help?'

Coach: That's great work. That's you, building relationships and building trust using the habits of benevolence. Now take it on for me. Let's assume you've built some trust and now you are going to evangelize. What would you say next?

Mark: [long silence] 'You know I've been up this tower before. I also felt nervous as I got near to the top, but then the sun suddenly came out and I saw this most amazing view across Paris and down to La Defense. I could see the Champs Elysees and Notre-Dame cathedral. I'd always dreamed of climbing the Eiffel Tower from when I was a little boy and, all of a sudden, I was there! I'll never forget that moment.'

Coach: That's pure evangelizing. How could anyone not be motivated to take the next step when listening to those words?

Mark: How about the third habit of benevolence; moral bravery. Where does that fit in?

Coach: Where do you think it fits in?

Mark: Well, how about this? I say to the guy, 'Look, my wife and I have been up the Eiffel Tower many times. You've got that huge backpack on you weighing you down. That can't be helping you. Why don't we stay here and look after your backpack and you go on to the top? What's more, we won't need these bottles of water, so you take one of these and that will keep you going. Just promise that you'll take a picture of the view from the top and show it to us when you get back here.'

Coach: Brilliant. You sacrifice your own goal, change your own plan, in order that he is more likely to be successful. That's brave! But would you do it?

Mark: [laughs] I'm not sure. Depends what mood I was in.

Coach: [laughs] I know what you mean. Now, let's come out of the analogy and return to the world of business. You've just proven to me that you know how to do both the theory and the practice of the habits of benevolence. How can you apply that experience to the challenge of building relationships in the boardroom?

Mark: We're all trying to climb our own Eiffel Tower; it's called our business plan. Some people are definitely getting nervous. I'm not sure its fear of heights, but probably fear of getting the sack or not hitting the bonus. Typically, I would be getting impatient and throwing my weight around at this point. However, I can see from our analogy how that might just make the problem worse. Sounds a bit radical, but I could be offering to help some of the others. Peter, in particular, is really struggling. I could let him drown, or I could step in and give him some time and energy and support. It's not my style, but maybe it is time to try something different.

Coach: It is just an experiment. It might work, it might not. But is it worth trying?

Mark: The feedback is clear. I need to develop these skills, otherwise one day I am going to be the one who is drowning. I may as well give it a go and then we can review the impact and take it from there.

Coach: What are you going to do then?

Mark: I don't want to plan it out in too much detail, because that's what I normally do and it takes away the spontaneous human touch. However, I know that, in the next couple of weeks, I will be in a meeting with Peter and I will have a choice as to whether to step in and support him, show him some benevolence, or sit back and watch him struggle. I want to make a promise to myself that when that moment comes I will choose to practise the habits of benevolence and then see what happens.

Coach: That's all you need to do. We can then review that experiment at our next coaching session and take it from there. Good luck with your next step!

In the above coaching session, Mark worked on all three of the habits of benevolence: choosing to be kind, to evangelize and to be morally brave. It would have been tempting for the coach to collude with his preferred mode of working and approach the challenge in a logical, analytical fashion. However, the introduction of a metaphor enabled Mark to bring his imagination and creativity to the fore. This helped him reframe the situation and break out of the silo of his competitive and task-driven mindset. He practises the skills in an imaginary situation and then brings the learning back into the world of business. At the end, he commits to experimenting with choosing to be kind, which he will then review at the next coaching session. Presenting the habits of benevolence as an experiment is often a realistic first step when working with deep-seated executive beliefs that might initially question the appropriateness of kindness as a core leadership skill.

Endnotes

1 Landau, S I (2000) *Cambridge Dictionary of American English* (Klett Edition), Ernst Klett Sprachen, Cambridge

2 Kawasaki, G (2015) The art of evangelism, *Harvard Business Review*, **93** (5), pp 108–11

3 Ibid

4 Sinek, S (2009) *Start with Why: How great leaders inspire everyone to take action, Penguin*, Harmondsworth

5 Niebuhr, R (1934) The serenity prayer, Cell, **801**, p 502

6 Hemingway, E (2012) *A Farewell to Arms*, The Hemingway Library Edition, Simon and Schuster, New York

7 Biswas-Diener, R (2012) *The Courage Quotient: How science can make you braver*, Wiley, Chichester

8 Lerner, J S and Keltner, D (2001) Fear, anger, and risk, *Journal of Personality and Social Psychology*, **81** (1), p 146

9 Rothbaum, B O, and Schwartz, A C (2002) Exposure therapy for posttraumatic stress disorder, *American Journal of Psychotherapy*, **56** (1), p 59

10 Guy, K and Guy, N (2003) The fast cure for phobia and trauma: evidence that it works, *Human Givens Journal*, 9 (4), pp 31–5

11 Cooper, L (2010) *Business NLP for Dummies*, Wiley, Chichester

12 Jeffers, S (2012) *Feel the Fear and Do it Anyway*, Random House, New York

13 Turing, A (1950) The Imitation Game. Computing machinery and intelligence, *Mind*, **49**

14 Harris, T (1969) *I'm Ok, You're Ok: A practical guide to transactional analysis*, Arrow Books, London

15 Webster, A (2003) *Polar Bear Pirates and Their Quest to Reach Fat City*, Random House, New York

16 Brown, B (2015) *Daring Greatly: How the courage to be vulnerable transforms the way we live, love, parent, and lead*, Penguin

06

Cracks in the pillars

What to do when things go wrong

Making mistakes

After reading Chapters 3–5, I hope you are suitably motivated to learn and apply the three pillars and nine leadership habits that inspire trust; but, in the real world, things go wrong. We make mistakes. Our best efforts fall short and our trustworthiness takes a hit. It could be that our abilities as a leader were not up to the task, our integrity is suddenly under question or we harmed others in pursuit of selfish goals. We wake up one morning and realize that one of the three pillars of trustworthiness has cracked. As one of the CEOs I interviewed put it: 'We don't live in a perfect world where honesty and trust are always 100 per cent achievable... it's how you deal with making mistakes that counts.'

This chapter acknowledges this fact and explores how best to cope with the inevitable cracks in our ability, our integrity and our benevolence as we further our executive careers. No one doubts that trust arrives on foot and leaves on horseback, but in my experience as a coach and leader, there are tools and techniques that can rebuild trust once it has been lost. The prescription will vary depending upon the pillar that is under scrutiny; in this chapter we will look at each in turn. However, prevention is better than cure. One factor above all acts as a frequent precursor to a breach of trust and that is stress. Stress may show up as excessive time pressure, tiredness, emotional sensitivity or inability to process information coherently. While a certain level of stress is a healthy pressure that optimizes our performance, there is a level of stress that overwhelms our capabilities. In this context, identifying and managing our stress levels becomes key to maintaining our reputation and our brand.

This truth was borne out by the 'Good Samaritan' experiments conducted by psychologists John Darley and Daniel Batson back in the early 1970s.[1] In their classic study, the research team recruited 67 students from the Princeton Theological Seminary and told them they were going to give a brief talk on the story of the Good Samaritan in a nearby building. However, while walking to the other office to give their talk, they would all pass a distressed man lying in a doorway, doubled over and coughing. Ironically, they would find themselves in the very situation of the Good Samaritan parable they were due to discuss. The researchers were interested in understanding how many students would stop to help the distressed man, particularly if they placed the students under different levels of stress. They varied the stress factor by giving each student one of the following three instructions:

1 *Low hurry:* 'It'll be a few minutes before they're ready for you, but you might as well head on over...'
2 *Medium hurry:* 'The assistant is ready for you, so please go right over.'
3 *High hurry:* 'Oh, you're late. They were expecting you a few minutes ago. We'd better get moving...'

Table 6.1 shows the percentage of people who stopped to help. The students who were under stress, ie thought that they were late, were much less inclined to show benevolence to the distressed man. Similarly, we know that our cognitive thinking ability drops when we are stressed and that we are more likely to act out of character, so risking issues of delivery and integrity in our work. This all conspires to undermine our trustworthiness in the eyes of others.

TABLE 6.1 Good Samaritan experiment results

Low Hurry	63%
Medium Hurry	45%
High Hurry	10%

FIGURE 6.1   Stress assessment

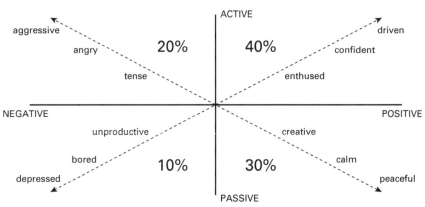

Sue Firth uses a simple model for managing stress in her book *Taking the Stress Out of Leadership*, which many of my coaching clients have benefited from.[2] Her work is based on a simple 2 × 2 matrix in which the vertical axis represents a range from passive to active energy and the horizontal axis represents the emotional state from negative to positive – see Figure 6.1. Each quadrant represents a different emotional and physical state that is characterized by different behavioural outcomes. For example, the upper right active and positive state will show up as an enthusiastic executive When experienced to a more extreme degree that enthusiasm will evolve into confidence and drive. The percentages in the figure reveal the ideal amount of time that an executive operating optimally would spend in each quadrant. It may seem like we should be spending 100 per cent of our time in the upper right quadrant, but this is both unsustainable and unlikely to be in the best interest of ourselves or those we lead.

STRESS LEVELS EXERCISE

To assess your own levels of stress, work with Figure 6.1 using the following questions:

- What percentage of your time do you typically spend in the upper right quadrant where you are active and positive?

- What percentage of your time do you spend in the lower right quadrant where you are passive and positive?

- What percentage of your time do you spend in the upper left quadrant where you are active and negative?

- What percentage of your time do you spend in the lower left quadrant where you are passive and negative?

- How do these percentages compare with one year ago?

- How do these percentages compare with the 'ideal' percentages shown in the figure?

- What are three actions you could take to shift the balance?

The above exercise will raise awareness of your current stress levels. Brave leaders take pre-emptive action to deal with stress before it undermines their trustworthiness. Ironically, that often involves being open and asking for help – a habit of integrity.

Mike Coup, CEO of UK supermarket group, Sainsbury plc, lost touch with his own stress levels with dramatic impact when conducting a media tour to promote the proposed £7bn merger of Sainsbury and Asda in April 2018.[3] During a break in an interview for the channel ITV, Mr Coup sat waiting patiently, not realizing that his own microphone was still on air. For reasons only known to himself, he then started warbling the words to the well-known song, 'We're in the Money' from the musical 42nd Street. It was not long in this transparent, 'red pill' world before a video of the incident hit social media and thousands watched aghast as a pale and sallow Mr Coup sang the words 'We're in the money, the sky is sunny, let's spend it, lend it, send it rolling along.' How could a CEO groomed in the art of media communications make such a jaw-dropping blunder? The day after, Mr Coup confessed that 'it had been an extremely stressful day and that maybe it was an unfortunate choice of song' before continuing to extol the stakeholder benefits of the proposed merger. That moment of stress had blotted Mr Coup's copybook for both honesty (Habit No. 4) and moral bravery (Habit No. 8). He had allowed himself to be stereotyped as a money-grabbing, self-serving leader who didn't care about the other stakeholders of the organization. In a final ironic twist, the UK regulator blocked the proposed merger and Mr Coup and his team did not end up 'in the money' after all. I'm sure Mr Coup is a perfectly decent man doing his best in a very difficult role but his story is a pertinent reminder to all leaders of the need to monitor and track our stress levels to make sure we are not at risk of similar high-profile lapses and mistakes.

I have worked with a number of senior leaders who are openly grappling with mental health issues and, thankfully, this topic is no longer the taboo that it once was. Being aware of and managing our stress levels prevents mistakes from happening. It is not necessarily about taking drastic action, though this is sometimes necessary, but it is always a case of taking decisive action. Importantly, taking care of our mental health involves being prepared to show some vulnerability and ask for help (Habit No. 5 – Choosing to be Open). That help may come from your boss, your team, an executive coach, or those in your personal life. There are always more people willing to help than we realize, yet it is down to us to take that courageous first step of recognizing there is a problem. Let us now consider the various cures for those difficult days when things do go wrong.

Cracks in Pillar 1: Ability

At the age of 27, I remember being summoned to the office of the then director of marketing of British Gas West Midlands. That day, it was a long walk down the hallowed corridors of power. The Director sat me down and I noticed he had a letter in his lap: 'John, I have received this five-page document from the Trade Union chief secretary regarding the new computer system you and your team have implemented in the region. And it is not a very pretty picture, is it?' He then proceeded to quote various passages from the letter as I sat there, crestfallen and mortified.

I still have a copy of that letter dated 23 July 1991. It starts with the ominous phrase 'universal disaster' and goes downhill from there. Most damning is the final page of the letter where I am accused of attributing the system problems to 'an act of God'. This is then followed by the phrase, 'To say that NALGO [the trade union] believes that the unbridled optimism of the project team is masking the problems... is an understatement.' In hindsight, I realize that in this particular case my evangelism may have got the better of me! It was hard to get sacked from British Gas at that time, but three months after this incident there was a reorganization of the business and I received a much shorter letter from the same director advising me that I had not been successful in applying for my own job! I'd gone from hot shot to hot potato in the space of six months. My trustworthiness took a dive, not due to my integrity or my benevolence, but because there was suddenly a crack in Pillar 1: can we trust him to deliver?

How do we handle it when we fail to deliver? The clue lies in what happened next in my own sorry tale. On the day that I received the letter advising me that I had not been successful in applying for my own job, my mentor and manager at the time, Graham Nye, took me for a drink. Graham had backed me at British Gas since I was a spotty 18-year-old. He'd been pivotal in awarding me a British Gas university scholarship, designing various graduate training programmes and appointing me as the youngest senior manager in the region at the age of 25. That day, I was crying in my beer bemoaning that my short career in British Gas was over and drowning in self-pity. Yet, Graham saw it differently. As I reeled off one morbid post-mortem after another, Graham kept saying, 'Yes, but think about what you've learnt'. Think of what I'd learnt! Learning was the last thing on my mind. At the time, I thought he was being grossly insensitive but, over the years, I have realized that he was giving me exceptionally wise counsel. For when Pillar 1 cracks the opportunity is to learn that failure is part of the process.[4] That day in 1991 I failed, but the learning from that failure laid the foundations for future success.

Michael Jordan, one of the greatest basketball players of all time, was referring to this lesson when he said:

> I have missed more than 9,000 shots in my career. I have lost almost 300 games. On 26 occasions I have been entrusted to take the game-winning shot and I missed. I have failed over and over again in my life. And that is why I succeed.

Failure is part of the process because failure triggers the opportunity to learn and learning leads to success. When our abilities and those of the teams we lead fail to deliver, there is only one antidote and that is to keep going. Keep going. Learn what you need to learn and try again. And it's not the end until you give in or you give up. Here are three failures who never gave up:

- Albert Einstein (Nobel Prize-winning physicist) – a child who did not speak until he was four years old and who was diagnosed by his teachers as having learning disabilities.
- James Dyson (inventor of the bag-less vacuum cleaner) – an entrepreneur who failed 3,000 times as he developed the prototypes for his award-winning product.
- J K Rowling (author of the Harry Potter novels) – a writer whose initial manuscript was rejected by 12 publishers.

Stephen Joseph has conducted some interesting research in this area.[5] The title of his book is taken from the Nietzsche quote, 'What doesn't kill us makes us stronger'. The book documents his research into the field of PTSD (post-traumatic stress disorder). Research into PTSD began in the 1980s. By the 1990s, researchers started to look at how trauma can sometimes be a catalyst for positive change and post-traumatic growth. It was found that after experiencing a traumatic event, people can report positive changes in the following areas:

- *Relationships:* people reported greater appreciation of friends and family.
- *Self-perception:* people accepted their vulnerabilities and weaknesses.
- *Life philosophies:* people re-evaluated what really mattered in their lives.

In 2004, a study found that 30 to 70 per cent of trauma survivors experienced such positive change.[6] These findings are prompting psychologists to reconsider whether PTSD always leads to a damaged and dysfunctional life; it may be a springboard to higher levels of psychological wellbeing. On a smaller scale, this research should prompt us to re-evaluate our own mini-traumas when we fail to deliver at work and damage our trustworthiness. In those moments, trusted executives keep going and seek the learning; don't live in the past, learn from it.

Alongside this ability to keep a sense of perspective, the CEOs I interviewed emphasized the importance of communication in recovering from a failure to deliver. There is a need to fix the things that went wrong as quickly as possible, but how the trusted executive communicates in this period will be critical in determining the long-term fall-out. Reflecting on a recent failed customer project, one CEO lamented as follows:

> We didn't communicate enough so the situation escalated. We should have been out there showing our understanding of the customer, showing that we understood the challenges, showing our commitment to solve those challenges and being transparent on the plans that we had to improve the situation. What annoys me is that we haven't got our act together in order to present the facts. So you end up in a situation where the client's perception is based on sentiment and hearsay.

This comment reminds us of the thin line between the 'unbridled optimism' of my earlier personal example and a focus on establishing the true facts of the situation then moving towards a progressive resolution. One step at a time we rebuild our trustworthiness by exceeding the client's own expectations. In such a scenario, clients can be extraordinarily forgiving.

In essence, when we experience a crack in one of the pillars of trustworthiness then, in the short term, we must lean on the other two to a greater degree. Often it is worth scanning the other leadership habits to assess which of these might come to our rescue. A good example of this occurred when my local train operator, Chiltern Railways, suffered a track landslide on their Birmingham to London route and failed to deliver the operating timetable for a period of six weeks.[7] When normal service was resumed, the first action that the company took was to reduce fares by 15 per cent. Most travellers regarded this as an act of integrity; they had caused considerable disruption and this was an honest act of compensation. However, as well as calling upon the habits of integrity, the train operator then exceeded itself by calling upon one of the habits of benevolence. For a week after the track re-opened, passengers were offered complimentary coffee. Passengers interpreted this as a random act of kindness (see Chapter 5). I travelled on one of those services that first week and, when the offer was announced, I looked around the train carriage to see a moment of delight on people's smiling faces. What a masterstroke! A great example of using the habits of benevolence and integrity to counter a failure in the habits of ability.

Cracks in Pillar 2: Integrity

A failure to deliver is one thing, but a failure in integrity strikes us at a different level. For most of us, it is harder to forgive acts of dishonesty, deception and arrogance than it is to forgive acts of incompetence. The difference lies in the intent behind the behaviour and is captured in the saying, 'As long as your intention is pure, your execution can be flawed.' In other words, if someone's motivation is to do a good job but they make a mistake, we judge them less harshly than if someone is highly competent yet intends to exploit us. This has significant implications for how we handle cracks in the pillar of integrity compared to cracks in the pillar of delivery.

Shortly after the publication of my first book, *Challenging Coaching*,[8] I received a request at short notice to be interviewed by the *Sunday Times*. It was a Sunday afternoon and the journalist wanted to speak to me before 4 o'clock. I was excited and also flustered because this phone call would interrupt a family occasion. Stress levels were rising. I remember pacing around my lounge answering the journalist's questions with little preparation. Still,

CRACKS IN THE PILLARS

I came off the call and felt reasonably satisfied with how it had gone. One hour later, I was walking with my family when it suddenly struck me that I had told a lie on the call. In the interest of simplicity and in my over-excited state, I had attributed a coaching example to myself rather than to a colleague to whom the event had actually happened. Not only that, but the colleague was a close friend who might well read the article when it appeared in the Sunday press. Pillar 2 was about to crack.

My heart started racing. What should I do? Part of me wanted to hope that the example would not be used in the article or it would never be published or my colleague would never get to find out. Part of me wanted to speak to the colleague to explain to him what had happened and ask him if he was ok that I used the story in that way. Part of me wanted to ring the journalist and tell her that I didn't want the article published at all. And then part of me, only a tiny part of me, wanted to eat humble pie. I focused on that tiny part and, as I did, it grew larger. I swallowed hard, picked up the phone, called the journalist and told her exactly what I'd done. It was a horrible 10 minutes. I felt ashamed. But I didn't die. The world carried on turning. The journalist accepted my apology and published the article without the incriminating example. It was a painful lesson in handling a crack in my own integrity.

Your own integrity crack may not involve talking to journalists on a Sunday afternoon, but it may involve one or more of these other common executive challenges:

- Speaking the truth, and nothing but the truth, in an interview for your dream job.

- Being brutally honest with a client whose business you are desperate to secure.

- Creating an all-staff announcement to justify an imminent round of redundancies.

- Issuing a press release to explain a downturn in business performance.

In each of these scenarios it is tempting to be economical with the truth, or worse. It was Rudy Giuliani, the former mayor of New York, who first coined the phrase, 'Hope is not a strategy'[9] and this is our first port of call when contemplating a crack in the pillar of integrity. We can be tempted to hope that no one will find out, no one will notice, no one will care. We can hope that it will all be ok in the end. But hope without action is a gambler's last resort. It risks compounding one crack in integrity with a further, bigger crack. Every lie that is told incurs a debt to the truth.[10] Sooner or later, that debt must be repaid. The later it is repaid, the higher the price to pay..

On the other hand, choosing to swallow our pride is a strategy. And though it doesn't taste good, it tastes a lot better than public humiliation. The problem with eating humble pie is taking the first bite. It's like one of those jungle challenges on reality TV programmes where the participants are sat in front of a glass of water and a varied collection of ants and centipedes. The challenge is to eat the cocktail of nasties. The glass of water is used to get the first multi-legged creature down the throat. Once you've survived that first gulp then washing a few more down becomes a lot easier. So what is the equivalent of that handy glass of water when it comes to recovering from a crack in integrity?

As in Chapter 5, when we discussed the habit of choosing to be kind, the techniques of TA (transactional analysis) can help us take that first step towards recovering from a breach in integrity. In particular, TA has an exercise known as 'trackdown', which was first documented by Tom and Amy Harris in their book *Staying Ok*.[11] Over the years, I have used this exercise hundreds of times to help me recover quickly from personal setbacks and disappointments. I have also seen it have a profound impact on my clients. It is, by far, the one coaching exercise that has had the most impact on my own personal development.

TRACKDOWN EXERCISE

To use the exercise, let us first remind ourselves of the TA model with its parent, adult and child ego-states; see Figure 6.2.

In a situation where there has been a lapse in integrity, the child ego-state experiences acute shame, the parent ego-state goes into a frenzy of judgement and the adult ego-state becomes paralyzed by the resulting parent-child battle. The likelihood is that no action will be taken and hope becomes our strategy. The trackdown exercise re-empowers the adult ego-state so that a proactive step can be taken. To complete the trackdown exercise we write down the answers to the following questions:

1 *What part of me hurts?* The answer to this question is always 'my child ego-state' but it helps to write this down because it allows you to realize that the truth is that you are hurting, but it is only part of you that is hurting.

FIGURE 6.2   Ego-states

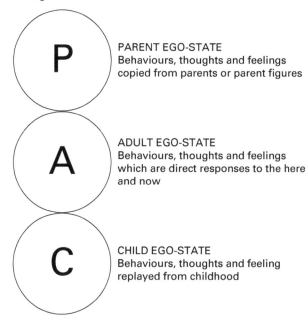

PARENT EGO-STATE
Behaviours, thoughts and feelings
copied from parents or parent figures

ADULT EGO-STATE
Behaviours, thoughts and feelings
which are direct responses to the here
and now

CHILD EGO-STATE
Behaviours, thoughts and feeling
replayed from childhood

2 *What feelings best describe my hurt?* Simply express the feeling or feelings as honestly and as openly as you can – for example, I feel ashamed and embarrassed, I feel gutted, I feel confused. This question is intended to validate your feelings so they are not denied or glossed over as inappropriate or not important.

3 *What happened in the recent past to trigger this feeling?* Be as specific as possible in tracking down the exact event that triggered the feeling, eg: 'It was when I realized that I had told a lie in the sales pitch about our pricing model.' The purpose of this question is to raise your awareness about the specific situations that 'push your buttons'. The more aware you can be of these, the more you can make conscious choices in the moment when they happen. (We will use the example of lying in a sales pitch for the remainder of the exercise.)

4 *What is my parent ego-state saying to me and how is my child ego-state responding?* Write this out as a script. For example:

Parent: 'You should have been honest.'
Parent: 'You should have prepared better for the sales pitch.'
Parent: 'You're totally out of your depth.'
Child: 'I want to run away.'

Child: 'I don't know what to do.'
Child: 'I want to give it all up.'

This script helps reveal the internal dialogue that has been triggered by the event. This dialogue is likely to be a repeating pattern built in childhood and reinforced through adult life. The script recognizes the reality of the internal battle but disempowers it through the act of writing it down and hence gaining a third-party perspective on the internal conversation. The more familiar you become with the dialogue, the more quickly you can intervene to disrupt its pattern.

5   *What situations in my past does this remind me of?* These could be recent situations or situations back in childhood. Again, the question helps you step back and gain perspective, because all these past events are now not as important as you thought they were at the time. In my example, it could be that the situation reminded me of stealing Simon's Jonty West hat in primary school, as mentioned in Chapter 4! My first defining lapse in integrity.

6   *What is another way of looking at this?* This question invites creativity and encourages a shift of perspective. Having allowed the child and parent ego-states to vent some of their emotion and judgement, we are now inviting the adult ego-state to make its first contribution. In my example, another way of looking at the situation might be that this was an opportunity to practise bouncing back from disappointments and set-backs.

7   *What is the adult ego-state analysis of the facts, risks and likely outcomes?* Now that the overwhelming feelings have been disempowered, we continue to let the adult ego-state take centre stage:

Fact: Our pricing policy was not on the agenda for this client meeting.
Fact: I am not perfect.
Fact: We are due to meet the client again next week.
Risk: I could rely upon hope as my strategy.
Risk: I could overreact and withdraw from the sale.
Risk: My integrity could be damaged significantly unless I take some action.
Likely outcome: I will take action to recover this situation.
Likely outcome: I will have to swallow my pride.
Likely outcome: It will not be the end of the world.

What now is my best reaction to this situation? We now ask the adult ego-state to plan the next steps. Note that sometimes the answer to this question may be to do nothing! In this example, the answer would be, 'I need to swallow my pride, pick up the phone, apologize to the client and re-present our pricing policy at the meeting next week.'

8 *What might I do differently if this situation happens again?* Again, we are engaging the adult ego-state to learn from what has happened and to seek closure on the experience. In my example, the answer could be, 'Next time I am asked a question by a client that I didn't expect, I need to say that I don't have an immediate answer, but I will get back to them within 24 hours with the answer'.

By using the trackdown exercise we can take action quickly to take the first steps to recover from an issue with our honesty, our openness or our humility. It is like emergency first aid applied at the scene of an accident. It stabilizes the situation and removes the immediate sense of panic. Through its application, we do not rely upon hope and we stem the impact on our trustworthiness.

Cracks in Pillar 3: Benevolence

You might think that a crack in the third pillar of benevolence is less critical than a crack in the other two pillars of ability and integrity. You might think that a lapse in benevolence can be shrugged off compared to failing to deliver or being dishonest. I would tend to agree that, in the short term, being cruel, being negative and being a moral coward do not immediately lead to serious organizational sanctions. The cracks in Pillar 3 tend to be hairline cracks that cluster together over a period of time. Initially barely noticeable, slowly but surely they weaken trustworthiness until one day the whole pillar crumbles into dust without an obvious cause. It is similar to when you get a small crack in your car windscreen. You carry on driving, sometimes for thousands of miles, then a small piece of grit kicks up from a lorry tyre, shatters the glass and leaves you gripping the wheel; startled and staring at fresh air. Losing Pillar 3 is 'death by a thousand cuts'.

For the same reasons, cracks in Pillar 3 do not tend to make the headlines. There is no dramatic story to tell; it is a sad and slow decline. One day, the executive leader leaves the building and no one notices. The atmosphere and culture of the office change, but nobody links it to one person's departure; they have already forgotten the leader's name. To be on the receiving end of such a fall from grace is like suffering a bereavement. It is like being Ebenezer Scrooge in Charles Dickens' *A Christmas Carol*.[12] The ghost of business past visits you in your dreams and shows you all the little digs you dished out to your team, all the cold water you poured on other people's ideas and all the moments you kept quiet to save your own skin. It leaves a bad taste in the mouth. Then you hear the ghost lamenting on your behalf, 'I wear the chain I forged in life… I made it link by link, and yard by yard; I girded it on of my own free will, and of my own free will I wore it.' Beware the hidden toll of cracks in Pillar 3!

If you worry that you might have picked up a touch of the Ebenezer Scrooges in your executive career, how do you correct that situation without relying upon ghoulish, nocturnal visits? Dickens' parable gives us a clue as to the starting point: honest feedback. For example, you could do worse than taking the DO HB CHECK questions from the end of Chapter 5 and circulating them to the members of your team. Ask them to answer the questions honestly and in confidence and then debrief the results with a qualified coach or trusted mentor. What story are they telling? Sometimes you will get a shock.

I was asked to carry out a similar exercise for a European managing director of a significant global business. This leader was highly intelligent and a man of high integrity. As a result, he wanted me to give him the honest truth. 'What do they *really* think of me?' he pleaded as we ran through the feedback in an airport hotel. 'They think you're a cold fish,' I replied. Clumsily, I had used an English idiom and I was met by a puzzled continental expression. 'A cold fish? What is that? Do I smell or something?' he replied. Now, I measured my words more carefully, 'When they use the term "cold fish" they mean that you come across as a hard-hearted individual who is distant and unfeeling.' At this point, I squirmed in my seat and stared at the coffee cup in front of me. The silence seemed to stretch and stretch and then, finally, he said calmly 'Yes, I am *the* cold fish.' His Pillar 3 was littered with hairline cracks, but he had made a massive first step in recovering that situation. Now, like Ebenezer Scrooge, he could at least start to grieve for his lost benevolence.

I do regard recovering benevolence as akin to a grieving process. In pursuing the best results at any cost, we can lose something precious in our humanity. When we suddenly realize this has happened, Elisabeth Kübler-Ross's 'stages of grief' model[13] can help us chart a forward course.

FIGURE 6.3   Kübler-Ross grief cycle

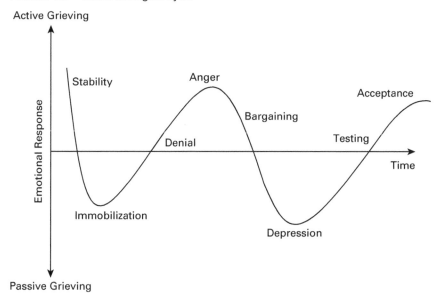

Kübler-Ross's work focused on helping terminally ill patients. She researched how people reacted when they lost a person close to them and suggested that it was common for people who are grieving to pass through the stages shown in Figure 6.3. The model has since been used to help people who are working through various traumas and changes. I have used it to support leaders who recognize they have lost the habits of benevolence. While each leader is different, the model does enable a discussion to take place about how they might navigate a journey to recover kindness, moral bravery and evangelism in their work. As an example, here are some interventions I might make in the different stages:

- *Immobilization:* 'I can imagine this feedback has come as a shock, so why don't I give you some time to digest it and we can discuss it when we next meet.'
- *Denial:* 'I know this is not how you see yourself, but how can you make sense of your colleagues' perceptions?'
- *Anger:* 'What's your side of the story here?'
- *Bargaining:* 'I know you don't fully agree with the feedback, but what do you think are the consequences of carrying on like this?'

- *Depression:* 'I can understand you feel like packing it all in. What can you do to take a break and get some perspective?'
- *Testing:* 'It's great that you have experimented with introducing some new initiatives to get closer to your colleagues.'
- *Acceptance:* 'Do you remember that time when I called you a "cold fish"? I think you could have throttled me, but I hope you are glad I was honest with you.'

I hope this brief foray into the world of recovering benevolence has demonstrated how unique it is compared to the other two pillars. Benevolence is an issue of the heart and, in that way, it is more complex and mysterious than the habits of ability and integrity. This is an area where I would expect more work will need to be done to support trusted executives in the red pill world. We are only in the foothills of exploring this topic yet the vision is for tomorrow's executive leaders to echo the parting words of Ebenezer Scrooge as he recovered his own benevolence:

> I will honour Christmas in my heart, and try to keep it all the year. I will live in the past, the present, and the future. The spirits of all three shall strive within me. I will not shut out the lessons that they teach![14]

POINTS TO PONDER

- You are not perfect. You have made mistakes. Think of one example from each pillar of trustworthiness where your own behaviour has fallen short of what you would expect. What were your levels of stress at the time? How did you recover the situation? What did you learn?

- Where are the risks for you, your team and your organization? Which of the three pillars of trustworthiness is currently under strain? What is the worst that could happen if you carry on exactly as you are? How might the other two pillars of trustworthiness come to your aid?

- This chapter has briefly introduced a number of coaching exercises and psychological models – Sue Firth's stress assessment, Stephen Joseph's work on post-traumatic growth, the TA trackdown exercise and Kübler-Ross's stages of grief. Which one of these made most impact on you? What are your next steps regards researching that work in more detail and putting it into practice?

- Are you brave enough to ask for honest feedback on your level of benevolence using the DO HB CHECK questions at the end of Chapter 5?

Endnotes

1 Darley, J M and Batson, C D (1973) From Jerusalem to Jericho: A study of situational and dispositional variables in helping behaviour, *Journal of Personality and Social Psychology*, **27** (1), p 100

2 Firth, S (2018) *Taking the Stress Out of Leadership: A practical guide to increasing well-being*, Sue Firth Publications

3 ITV News (2018) Sainsbury's CEO Apologises for singing 'We're in the Money' between Asda merger interviews, https://www.itv.com/news/calendar/2018-04-30/itv-news-exclusive-sainsburys-ceo-sings-were-in-the-money-before-asda-merger-interview/ (archived at https://perma.cc/KG7T-WU4R)

4 Day, I (2014) Failure is part of the process, *Challenging Coaching*, http://challengingcoaching.co.uk/failure-is-part-of-the-process/ (archived at https://perma.cc/JG23-SLXH)

5 Joseph, S (2011) *What Doesn't Kill Us: The new psychology of posttraumatic growth*, Basic Books, New York

6 Linley, P A and Joseph, S (2004) Positive change following trauma and adversity: A review, *Journal of Traumatic Stress*, **17** (1), pp 11–21

7 BBC (2015) Chiltern rail line reopens after 350,000 tonne landslip, *BBC News*, 13 March

8 Blakey, J and Day, I (2012) *Challenging Coaching*, Nicholas Brealey, London

9 Strachan, M (2009) Managing change proactively within the current HIM professional domain, *Health Information Management Journal*, **38** (3), p 7

10 Wakeford, R (2020) *Chernobyl*, Home Box Office (HBO)/Sky Atlantic television mini-series

11 Harris, A B and Harris, T A (2011) *Staying Ok*, Random House, London

12 Dickens, C (1843) *A Christmas Carol*, Simon and Schuster, London

13 Kübler-Ross, E (2009) *On Death and Dying: What the dying have to teach doctors, nurses, clergy and their own families*, Taylor & Francis, London

14 Dickens, C (1843) *A Christmas Carol*, Simon and Schuster, London

PART THREE

Building a high-trust culture

In Part I of this book, we reflected on how authority had become a surrogate for trust in the blue pill world. We contemplated how the red pill of transparency breaks down that model and so transforms the purpose of business and the role of the executive leader. A sole focus on profit is gradually being replaced by a triple focus on results, relationships and reputation. The executive leader, traditionally an untrustworthy agent, is evolving into a trusted steward. In the red pill world, executive leaders inspire trust in those around them by role-modelling the three pillars of ability, integrity and benevolence.

In Part II, we plunged into the detail of the three pillars to explore the practicalities of the nine leadership habits that inspire trust. Our focus was the individual executive and how he or she develops new awareness and skills in the areas of delivery, coaching, consistency, honesty, openness, humility, evangelism, bravery and kindness. Chapter 6 maintained this focus on the individual executive by acknowledging that sometimes we make mistakes and damage trust, and covered the strategies for recovering quickly from those setbacks.

Now, in Part III, we consider how to 'walk the talk' with the Nine Habits of Trust. It is here we will look to convert the theory into practice because, at heart, I am a businessman not an academic. For the same reason, it was memorable to host the launch of the first edition of this book at the National Liberal Club in April 2016, but it was even more rewarding to be back at the same venue over three years later to announce the winner of our first 'Trusted Executive of the Year' award – Russell Atkinson, CEO of NAHL

Group plc. That evening, the Trusted Executive Foundation gathered over 20 CEOs and board-level leaders who had worked with the Nine Habits of Trust in their organizations. We heard how each had put the theory into practice and brought the model to life in different ways. This section distils the learnings of their experience for those who wish to tread the same path.

Some of those leaders had hosted a 'Trusted Executive' workshop for their executive team; some had conducted a Nine Habits leadership survey; some had been on the receiving end of a Nine Habits 360 feedback report; some had been coached on specific habits as they pursued their triple bottom line goals. All of them had committed to taking the next step to becoming Trusted Executives. It was a special evening and it reminded me how much had happened since the original publication of the book. Back then, I didn't know that the Chartered Management Institute would shortlist the first edition of the book as its business book of the year. I didn't know that I would go on to deliver over 100 keynote speaker sessions and workshops on the Nine Habits of Trust to thousands of leaders across Europe, the United States, Canada, the Middle East and Asia. I didn't know that the *FT*, the *Sunday Times* and BBC News would feature the work and that the BBC2's iconic 'Daily Politics' show would invite me for an interview. That was all a twinkle in the eye back in 2016!

It isn't just my world that has changed dramatically since the publication of the first edition of this book. Back then, I would love to have predicted that the UK would vote to leave the EU and that Donald Trump would be elected US president, but I didn't. I would love to have predicted the rise of the #MeToo movement, the championing of climate change by Greta Thunberg and the abrupt arrival of COVID-19 as a global disruptor, but I didn't. The context of leadership has changed dramatically since 2016. All of these trends have reinforced my conviction that trust, not power, must increasingly become the currency of our leadership. Only high-trust cultures will provide the psychological safety that the modern stakeholder demands.

As highlighted in Chapter 2, the most encouraging business shift since 2016 has been the increasingly rapid switch from the single bottom line agency theory model to the triple bottom line stewardship model of business. The most surprising advocates of this new model have come from the investor community where the staid world of ethical investing has metamorphosed into the mainstream adoption of ESG (environmental, societal, governance) factors as the new benchmark for prudent investment decisions. In their annual tours of investment fund presentations, CEOs are now routinely grilled on their approach to sustainability, climate change, diversity, executive remuneration, gender pay gaps and social justice considerations. It is, indeed, an exciting time to be a CEO!

In the next chapter, I will collate the learning from all these experiences of putting the theory of trust into practice. First, we will look at how leaders have used the Nine Habits model to work on their trust behaviours and to build high-performing teams. Next, we will consider the role of measurement in building a high-trust culture, partly through the setting of triple bottom line goals and also through using the Nine Habits model to measure trust as a KPI (key performance indicator). Finally, I will offer some advice for leaders on how to use the Nine Habits model to meet the demands of city analysts who are increasingly assessing your brand reputation and risk profile using environmental, societal and governance (ESG) factors.

07

Working with the Nine Habits of Trust

For many of us, it is common sense to think that the behaviour of senior leaders sets the tone for the rest of the organization. As part of my doctoral research at Aston Business School, I wanted to put this notion to the test. Would it stand true under the weight of academic scrutiny? Having finished the research, I can now report it is a scientific truth that the trustworthy behaviour of CEOs and their teams is a significant predictor of the perceived trustworthiness of the organizations they lead. If you are a leader, you're behaviour matters. It does start with you. At the Trusted Executive Foundation, our focus is on the behaviour of the CEO and the senior leadership team because we know if we can inspire those executives to role-model the Nine Habits of Trust then the rest of the organization will inevitably follow. It is the single biggest key to building a high-trust culture.

Unfortunately, I can also confirm from my research that the very same CEOs and leaders whose behaviour is so important have a much rosier perception of their trustworthiness than the people whom they lead. Typically, CEOs rate themselves 29 per cent more trustworthy than others do. Also, they assess their organizations as being 23 per cent more trustworthy than others do.[1] I call this difference the 'authenticity gap'. In other words, the larger the gap in perceptions, the more the CEO and senior team risk fooling themselves that they are doing an excellent job with inspiring trust relative to the more negative views of employees, customers and other stakeholders. In a transparent world, this authenticity gap will be exposed and, once exposed, it will damage personal and brand reputation. Stakeholders are ruthlessly cynical and will quickly savage those leaders and organizations that they suspect of 'trust-washing' when the actions do not match the words.

Given their importance, I have been studying CEOs and their teams around the world very carefully since the first publication of this book. I have sought them out through coaching assignments, interviews, keynote speaker sessions and workshops. Through these engagements, I have been able to ask them many questions and listen to their opinions. I have heard their views on trust and invited them to grapple with the Nine Habits model in their leadership. In the next section, I will summarize the key themes and insights that have emerged from these various discussions in the hope they will give you a fast-track opportunity to absorb their learning and wisdom.

Broken systems, difficult job descriptions and Donald Trump

In 2016, when I first started delivering half-day workshops to CEOs on the topic of The Trusted Executive, I would allocate the first hour of the session to convince the attendees that there was a trust crisis in leadership, ie that there was a problem for which we needed a solution. At the end of that time, I would still have a few die-hard cynics who would shrug their shoulders and roll their eyes. 'We'll just carry on as we are, thanks very much' seemed to be the message from their body language. Contrast this with a workshop I delivered to 15 CEOs in December 2019. I was 20 minutes into the session and carefully building the case for change when one of the attendees banged the table abruptly and exclaimed, 'John, what you're telling us is that the system is fundamentally broken. We all know that and we want to know what to do about it!' I felt like asking if he could wait a further 40 minutes as we hadn't got to that stage of the session yet, but the experience demonstrated to me that attitudes had shifted. The case for change is no longer tentative; it is compelling. CEOs may not have worked out how to deal with the trust problem, but they certainly know it exists.

A similar Eureka moment occurred in another workshop when the attendees were discussing the webcam video of Travis Kalanick, ex-CEO of Uber, arguing with one of his drivers late at night (the case study featured in Chapter 4). Some were appalled at Travis's arrogance and casual rudeness to the driver; others thought the driver had mistreated him. One of the CEOs present challenged me saying, 'John, are you saying that we need to behave as if we are on video 24 hours a day?' 'Yes', I replied. 'Well, that's a difficult job description, isn't it?' he railed. 'Yes, it is', I replied, 'and if you don't want the job then don't apply for it.' It was a blunt reply on my part but it made the point. In a world where nothing can be hidden, the CEO is subject to radical transparency. Some say it is not fair, but it is the reality and, as the old saying goes, 'If you fight with reality, reality tends to win!'

My final nugget from the CEO workshops came from a session I delivered in Boston, USA in August, 2017.[2] It was the first CEO workshop of a number I was delivering that week and I had been wrestling with whether to use Donald Trump as the case study exercise for the Nine Habits of Trust. In the end, I decided to go for it and once I'd carefully explored the model with an attentive, enthusiastic audience, I clicked for the next slide and a picture of Donald Trump appeared in the centre of the enormous screen at the front of the room. 'How do you think this leader would fare against the Nine Habits that inspire trust?' I asked. The words hung in the air like a stale odour, the silence was deafening. I stared at my shoes and quietly counted to 10. Then a courageous soul piped up, 'I think Donald Trump is brave'. 'Yes', I said, 'whatever you might think of his opinions I don't think anyone can say that Donald Trump is not a master at Habit No.8; being brave.' With the ice broken, I pressed on, 'What other strengths does he have?' 'Trump's open, what you see is what you get,' offered a voice from my left. 'Yes', I replied, 'you might not like what he tweets at 3am, but we could all agree that he is not hiding anything; he excels at Habit No.4; being open.' 'And Trump's certainly delivered in the world of business' suggested a lady at the back of the room. 'Yes', I agreed, 'he got the deals done in his business career and people were so tired of mainstream politicians who hadn't delivered on their promises that enough voters were willing to give him a chance of delivering in the world of politics.' We were on a roll, so I upped the ante, 'Now, how about his weaknesses? What are the habits that undermine trust in Donald Trump?' Silence. More inner counting. 'Well, can anyone say that he is humble?' asked a guy pointing at Habit No.6 in the diagram of the model. 'And how about Habit No.2; being consistent?' offered his colleague, 'The best he can do on that one is being consistently inconsistent.' Laughter broke the tension. What a relief! I ventured to summarize:

> As a researcher on trust, what I find fascinating about Donald Trump is that he is much stronger on the Nine Habits than many would expect him to be. If you focus on how he behaves, rather than what he says, you can quickly identify the habits where, compared to traditional establishment politicians, he scores highly: being brave, evangelizing, being open, delivery, being honest. Like all of us, he has his blind spots – coaching, being consistent, being humble – but,

overall, Donald Trump breaks the mould of the traditional, and mistrusted, establishment leaders.

By assessing Donald Trump, these CEOs realized that we all have strengths and weaknesses when it comes to the Nine Habits. As one of our clients put it, 'The fact is there are nine habits and you can't hit them all, all of the time, because we're all fallible human beings. You are going to get it wrong along the way.' These insights free leaders to be honest about their own Nine Habits self-assessment, which is the exercise that concludes all our introductory workshops.

The Nine Habits self-assessment

The same self-assessment questionnaires that feature earlier in this book have been used by hundreds of leaders in workshops around the world. Typically, we allocate the final hour of a half-day workshop for the participants to complete the questionnaire and then work together in pairs to debrief the outcomes and learnings. I challenge each participant to write down the one habit that has the potential to make the most positive impact on their performance. Finally, I ask them to write down one action that they will complete during the week after the workshop to demonstrate their commitment to building the muscle of their chosen habit. At that point, I remind them, 'A journey of a thousand miles begins with a single step. It is the only way it can begin.' Having completed this exercise, we hold a final plenary session in the workshop where the participants share their chosen habits and committed actions. That discussion is often illuminating and inspiring. Here are some snippets from these discussions we have captured over the years:

- Habit No.8 – Choosing to be brave
  'I took away the habit to be Brave, which is what's brought me here today. We work in the financial markets, so trust is huge and it's also very difficult to understand. So, the whole being brave point was to get everyone together to talk about it' – Managing Director, financial services sector.

- Habit No.1 – Choosing to deliver
  'My habit was around Delivery. I found it really useful to use that awareness to share with your team what you're trying to focus on.

It makes a real difference. It allows a common conversation; it allows a common language' – Strategy Director, public sector.

- **Habit No.7 – Choosing to evangelize**
  'I took away the habit to Evangelize. My habit now is to talk more about the good things that we're doing in the business. You've got no choice but to evangelize, or you're not going to take anyone on that journey with you' – Managing Director, professional services sector.

Over the years, I have picked up some patterns which may be of benefit to those of you striving to practise these habits in your leadership. Firstly, in our workshops, no one has ever volunteered to focus on Habit No.4 – choosing to be honest. No one has ever wanted to be the dishonest person in the room! Does this mean that all the participants attending our workshops have never lied, exaggerated the truth or tolerated dishonesty in others? No, it simply means that dishonesty is the behaviour which triggers the most shame in us. Morally, dishonesty is the habit we have the most difficulty accepting. We would rather admit to being unkind, or not delivering, or not being brave than being dishonest. And yet, 51 per cent of employees believe they have been lied to by their colleagues.[3] We know dishonesty exists in business and each one of us. Our reluctance to talk about dishonesty risks driving this behaviour into the shadows where it festers unnoticed. It also risks letting dishonest leaders avoid accountability because we are frightened to tackle this issue in our teams or our organizations. I hope that over time we can become braver to face up to the honesty challenge and share our struggles with it more openly.

The second insight from these workshop discussions is on the topic of personality types. I have learnt that extroverts are more likely to want to focus on the habits of being humble, being consistent and being kind, whereas introverts wish to improve their openness, their bravery to speak up and their confidence to evangelize. In another aspect of diversity, it is men that are most likely to struggle with Habit No.9 – choosing to be kind. Often male leaders have been conditioned to be strong and ruthless. Even though they may be kind in their personal lives, many men have learnt to leave their kindness at home rather than bring it into the workplace. At the end of one workshop with 100 leaders from a hospital trust, everyone filed out of the room leaving one man sat at his table looking confused. I approached him and said, 'Are you ok?' He replied, 'I've just realized kindness is part of leadership.' I quizzed him further and asked, 'What job do you do in the hospital?' He said, 'I'm a doctor.' This confession worried me, but then he brilliantly clarified the situation by saying, 'I've always known I needed to be kind to be a great doctor, but I never knew I needed to be kind to be a great leader.' It's a great day when you feel you are permitted to be kind.

Continuing the theme of diversity, I find that women often focus on Habit No.8 – choosing to be brave. Their conditioning has often involved being admonished for speaking up, or for leading from the front, in traditionally male-dominated environments. I find that the Nine Habits model enables leaders to discuss these gender-related topics with curiosity and understanding without the conversation descending into judgement, labels and personal offence. Models can provide a more empowering platform from which to explore difference. I hope the Nine Habits will continue to act as a catalyst for these critical conversations in the future.

A final aspect of diversity relates to country culture. Much is written about behavioural differences in international business settings. When it comes to the Nine Habits, having delivered workshops all around the globe, I can share my own experience. As a rule of thumb, as I go west from the UK, I find the habits of being open, evangelizing and being brave get stronger. On the other hand, as I go east, I find the habits of being humble, being consistent and being kind get stronger. This subjective view aligns well with some recent academic research on the topic by Jeanne Brett and Tyree Mitchell, summarized in the *Harvard Business Review* article, 'How to Build Trust with Business Partners from Other Cultures'.[4] These researchers found that western cultures were typically more open to taking the risk of trusting others and they also identified a second factor that they termed the relative 'tightness' or 'looseness' of the culture. In a tight culture, people monitor social behaviour carefully and violations of social norms are discouraged. Using this definition, western cultures are typically looser and eastern cultures usually tighter. Therefore, the socially attractive habits of being humble, consistent and kind become more relevant to the trust equation as you go east, whereas in the West we are more prone to want to 'get down to business', leaving social niceties for later.

One of the most valuable outcomes of discussing the self-assessment of the Nine Habits in our workshops is that it demonstrates no one personality type, no one gender and no one country culture has perfected trust. As such, it is a great leveller. It enables us to discuss this vague, abstract and emotive word 'trust' in a more specific, objective and practical fashion. Often, the discussions help leaders grasp that, while no one leader can be perfect, a team can be perfect because a diverse team can have members who all excel at different habits.

Building a high-performance team

In 2016, Google published the results of Project Aristotle, a two-year study into the factors that produced the highest-performing teams inside the Google organization. When all the factors from 180 teams had been weighed and considered, it surprised the researchers to find that one factor above all characterized the top-performing teams. That factor was not individual skills, or team structure, or team longevity, or expert management – it was psychological safety.[5] Psychological safety is a 'shared belief held by members of a team that the team is safe for interpersonal risk-taking.' And what is the key ingredient that produces that feeling of psychological safety? It is the magic wand of trust. Similarly, many of you will be familiar with the work of Patrick Lencioni captured in his excellent book *The Five Dysfunctions of a Team*.[6] Lencioni lays out in the form of a pyramid the five factors that most seriously undermine team performance. The factor that a team must tackle before all others lies at the base of the pyramid – 'absence of trust'. In his book, Lencioni states, 'Trust is the foundation of real teamwork.' Only after building trust can the team move on to tackle the other four dysfunctions, but how do you build trust into the team in the first place?

Given the findings of Project Aristotle, Lencioni's work and other similar studies that highlight the role of trust in building high-performing teams, there is an opportunity to use the Nine Habits model for this purpose. A number of the clients of The Trusted Executive Foundation have pioneered using the model in this way. We have also used the model to build our team and within our Trusted Executive Fellowship Board CEO peer groups. From this experience, we can share various insights and learnings.

Our clients have found that different applications of the Nine Habits model are appropriate depending upon the maturity of the team. For example, using the Nine Habits 360 feedback tool requires a team that has already built a solid foundation of trust, whereas using the Nine Habits leadership survey is effective for new teams that are at the start of their journey together. It helps to think of Tuckman's model of team development to explore this aspect further. Tuckman suggested all teams go through four stages – forming, storming, norming and performing.[7] In the forming stage, the team is new, conversations are polite and there is much optimism about future possibilities. In this stage, we recommend conducting a Nine Habits leadership survey to diagnose the current reality of the organizational culture (see next section). This survey provides an initial benchmark and helps the team members become fluent in the model before they engage in more challenging conversations. Also, the team can channel its early enthusiasm into developing a clear and inspiring set of triple bottom line goals. As Covey said, starting with the end in mind is key.[8] Habit No.5, choosing to evangelize, comes to the fore in this stage. The sooner the team starts to visualize success along the three dimensions of results, relationships and reputation, the better equipped they will be for the later team development stages. The following client quotes highlight this point:

> 'One of the key things that we've changed is our vision. So, our vision statement is one thing, but our vision in terms of metrics and everything else has changed. We had the 2020 vision, which was very financially oriented. And for 2025 we put in a triple bottom line vision about results, relationships and reputation.' – CEO, distribution sector

> 'You can break the triple bottom line down into each department. So, a depot can have its targets for those areas. Even a department like HR, IT or Finance could have their results, relationships and reputation objectives, eg purchasing can measure their relationships with suppliers rather than customers.' – CEO, food retail sector

As the team matures and moves into the storming stage, members find that the honeymoon period is over, egos clash, frustrations build and deeper problems rise to the surface. It becomes key for the team to navigate difficult conversations and name the 'elephant in the room'. The integrity habits of openness, honesty and being humble are critical in this stage. We find it is often helpful for the team to have an independent Nine Habits coach to join their meetings and facilitate reflections on how the Nine Habits are showing up in their conversations. The team checks in against the model at the beginning and end of each meeting while the coach supports and challenges them, highlighting examples of good trust habits and identifying other habits that need to improve. The storming stage is inevitable in the development of every high-performing team, but leaders can navigate it more smoothly when supported by the Nine Habits model. Below are the reflections from leaders who have used the model in this way:

'I think if there's one habit our team still need to improve on it is openness. As we've gone through the programme, we've called it the elephant in the room and the elephant has sat there meeting after meeting and we all know it's there, but we dance around it.' – CEO, charity sector

'Our ability to talk through tough situations improved because of the openness and honesty we've taken from the programme. It has helped us to navigate some choppy water better.' – Strategy Director, public sector

'We use the Nine Habits model in all of our meetings. We start our meetings with it and finish with it as well. We really have seen the change in behaviour through the team by using it. I think we have seen a building of trust across the executive body.' – Executive Team Member, hospital trust

As the team reaches the calmer waters of Tuckman's norming stage, behaviours are becoming more predictable and team members are collaborating more closely. Habits 2 and 3 become more important – choosing to coach and choosing to be consistent. The team is becoming more self-sufficient, allowing the external coach to step back and one of the internal team to step forward and become the 'Nine Habits Champion'. The Nine Habits Champion is now responsible for the regular 'check-ins' at team meetings and organizes monthly calls with each team member to invite them to score their Nine Habits. In these calls, the Nine Habits Champion challenges team members to identify the habit, and associated behaviour, where they would most value the support of the rest of the team. In the team meetings, members share their chosen habit and get 'feedforward' from other members. Rather than feedback on their past behaviour, feedforward involves each team member giving one piece of advice on improving the habit in the future. It is a powerful exercise for building habit capabilities over time as noted by the following comments:

'Each individual works on their habits and then we come together and talk about them. I think the individual coaching support wraps around that and having that support been really, really helpful.' – Strategy Director, public sector

'As a leadership team, we recognized that we weren't doing enough coaching. I've got a team around me who are all very good. I direct them and motivate them and whatever, but then I don't necessarily spend enough time coaching them in terms of how to improve.' – CEO, food retail sector

Finally, the team evolves into the 'performing' stage of the Tuckman model. The team delivers tasks efficiently and effectively. They diagnose problems and resolve these quickly. Measuring strong progress towards triple bottom line goals boosts morale. The space is psychologically safe and the team is ready to use the Nine Habits 360 feedback tool. Each member collects detailed feedback from superiors, peers, team members and clients related to each of the Nine Habits. An accredited Nine Habits coach debriefs the confidential 16-page 360 feedback report with each of them to identify the learning and insights. Development plans and actions are agreed. At their next team meeting, members share the headlines from their own 360 feedback. They also review the consolidated 360 feedback for the team using specialized reports from the 360 feedback tool. These conversations dig deep and trigger new levels of openness, bravery and honesty in the team.

Figure 7.1 shows the summary chart from the 360 feedback report of a UK Managing Director (MD). The solid dots show the MD's self-perception against each habit. The open circles show the average perception of all the other respondents, which would have comprised the immediate manager, peers and team members. From the chart, we can see that the MD has a blind spot on the habits of being open and being consistent, where they regard themselves as more competent in these habits than do others. In the opposite case, we can see that they have hidden strengths on the habits of being humble, being kind and evangelizing where others have scored them higher on these habits than they have scored themselves. The remainder of the report drills down into the detail behind the scoring in line with other 360 feedback best practice. The report also includes free-format text feedback on each habit, which is often extremely valuable to help the leader take specific actions and development steps.

FIGURE 7.1   Summary chart individual 360 Nine Habits feedback

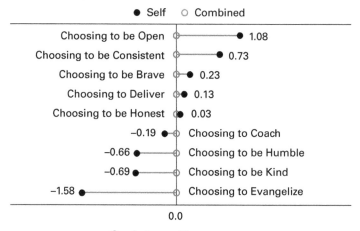

Gap between Mean scores

The summary chart in Figure 7.2 shows the consolidated 360 feedback for an executive leadership team in the public sector. The top left quadrant shows the three behaviours where the team is collectively strong. These behaviours are from the habits of being consistent and being honest. The numbers inside the circles indicate the number of team members who have the behaviour as a strength. The bottom left quadrant shows the three responses where the team is collectively weak. In this case, the answers are from the habits of being consistent, being kind and being open. The top right quadrant shows the one behaviour where the team collectively underrated itself relative to other people's perceptions, ie 'Is resilient to bounce back quickly from disappointments'. In this case, the behaviour was from the evangelize habit. The bottom right quadrant shows the two responses where the team has a potential blind spot, ie where they rated themselves higher than others did. In this case, the behaviours are from the habits of being open and being humble. Typically, the team would discuss this chart and other more detailed findings with their team coach and develop shared action plans to work on specific behaviours.

FIGURE 7.2   Summary chart team 360 Nine Habits feedback

As they have journeyed through Tuckman's stages using the Nine Habits model, the team has had to balance the professionalism of the ability habits (deliver, coach, be consistent), the character-based nature of the integrity habits (be honest, be open, be humble) and the collective ethos of the

TABLE 7.1 Tuckman stages and the Nine Habits model

	Forming	Storming	Norming	Performing
Tools	Nine Habits leadership survey Development of triple bottom line goals	Triple bottom line dashboard Nine Habits feedforward Nine Habits check-in	Triple bottom line dashboard Monthly Nine Habits review calls	Nine Habits 360 feedback Review of triple bottom line goals
Roles	Workshop facilitator	External team coach	Nine Habits champion	Individual coaches
Resources	Trusted Executive book	E-learning support – blogs, articles, case studies		
Workshops	Team Workshop 1		Team Workshop 2	Team Workshop 3

benevolent habits (evangelize, be brave, be kind). It's been an intense experience and one that has bonded the team deeply. They are delivering excellent results, having lots of fun and growing together as leaders. The group of competent yet competing individuals has become a high-performing, high-trust team. The process is summarized in Table 7.1.

What gets measured is treasured

We know that role-modelling and leading by example are potent levers in creating a high-trust culture. However, there comes the point where progress will stall unless the organization's goals and measurement systems adapt to align with the focus on the triple bottom line and trust as the new currency of leadership. In the blue pill world, organizations focused on the financial measures of success such as profit, return on capital employed, net asset value, etc. These were the raw ingredients of business planning and goal-setting. In the red pill world, more and more organizations will express their vision through triple bottom line goals. The following quote from one of our clients neatly captures this point:

> 'One of the key things that we've changed is our vision. We had the 2020 vision, which was very financially oriented. And for 2025, we put in a triple bottom line vision about results, relationships and reputation. For our triple bottom line, we're aiming for 9.5 per cent EBITDA margin, 95 per cent employee engagement and 95 per cent customer retention. We don't like to make it too complicated!' – CEO, distribution sector

In the Trusted Executive Foundation, we have our own triple bottom line vision. We are a not-for-profit start-up organization. Our 10-year plan is to gift over £1 million to UK-based Christian charities that are inclusive at the point of need. That is our measure of results. In parallel, our 'relationships' measure is to track the learning, inspiration and motivation of our team members through a monthly check-in in which every team member scores out of 10. We aim to achieve an 8 out of 10 average for this key performance indicator (KPI). Finally, we measure our reputational success via the number of hits to our website, which we see as a measure of how successful we are being at raising the profile of the work that we do.

In the same way that triple bottom line visions were rare in the blue pill world, the concept of trust was much spoken about but rarely measured and certainly not tracked as a KPI. In my interviews with CEOs, I asked them how they measured trustworthiness in their organizations. Here is a selection of their comments:

> 'I don't think there is a measure. There certainly isn't a single measure.'

> 'We have a scorecard. While trust is not a component on the scorecard, we view the customer and employee satisfaction metrics as a measure of our trust. These are proxy measures for trust.'

> 'Trust is the way an individual feels, so it is not something that can be easily measured.'

There was not one company in my research sample that had a direct measure for trust and yet all the executives interviewed agreed it was critical to their success. Comments in other studies such as the Populus white paper 'The Trust Deficit', reinforce these findings.[9] In this report, the authors concluded that 'business leaders viewed trust largely as a matter of personal judgement'. One FTSE 100 chairman says, 'I hadn't thought about trying to measure trust,' and another of his peers agrees, 'It's probably a bit difficult to say how do you actually measure [trust]'. Against this backdrop, is it surprising that, without leading indicators of trust levels, it risks slowly leaking away? The business carries on as usual until one day a newspaper headline hits hard and cartwheels the organization into a trust-related crisis.

In this book, we have reviewed case studies of organizations hit by a trust crisis – Uber, United Airlines, Facebook. If these organizations had set goals for trust and measured progress against a 'trust index' prior to their troubles, would this have picked up the erosion of stakeholder trust? This 'trust index' could have acted as a leading indicator, providing advance warning of the strategic risks that were building up in those businesses and prompting leaders to take proactive action. The impact of trust failure is specific and dramatic. In what other areas of business would we accept such lax, woolly thinking when it comes to measuring and tracking such a critical variable? If we are to treasure trust, then it is time to blow away the myth that it cannot be measured, any more than product quality, employee engagement or shareholder value cannot be measured. These are all high-level concepts that will yield to measurement if we consider them important enough to scrutinize and deconstruct.

One of the key objectives of my research on trust at Aston Business School was to fill this gap in our understanding of trust. As a result of the many hours interviewing and surveying CEOs and their teams, followed by an in-depth statistical analysis of the resulting data, the Nine Habits model emerged. The research then went further to create the first behavioural measurement tool for trust based on the Nine Habits. The 27 behaviours are the same as those presented earlier in this book as the self-assessment questionnaires at the end of the chapters on ability, integrity and benevolence. The Trusted Executive Foundation has converted the same 27 behaviours into the online Nine Habits leadership survey referred to earlier in this chapter. The survey takes four minutes to complete and we have now collected thousands of responses measuring trust across various organizations. We are now able to create a trust index for any organization and benchmark it against our broader sample. In the next section, we will share the findings of this tool with you.

Nine Habits leadership survey – benchmark data

The first question in the survey assesses the perceived importance of trust, the second question focuses on perceptions of organizational trust, and the final question uses the Nine Habits model to assess perceptions of leadership trust. As you review our survey findings below, I hope you can see how a 'trust index' could quickly be developed and assessed with each of your stakeholder groups – suppliers, customers, staff, shareholders, and the public at large. Such a 'trust index' could be reported every quarter. It could be the basis of setting goals that support triple bottom line success and it could be a prescient indicator of any looming reputational risk.

Survey question 1 – perceptions on the importance of trust

FIGURE 7.3   How critical is trust to the following business outcomes?

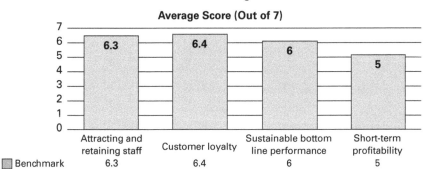

	Attracting and retaining staff	Customer loyalty	Sustainable bottom line performance	Short-term profitability
Benchmark	6.3	6.4	6	5

The benchmark data in Figure 7.3 highlights that senior leaders regard trust as essential to a variety of different stakeholder outcomes affecting employees, customers and investors. Trust is even viewed as critical to short-term profitability by the vast majority of respondents even though this is an area where leaders can be tempted to trade off trust against other competing variables. The views of the survey respondents are in line with those arising from other academic research and confirm that trust is a magic wand that can deliver a multitude of positive outcomes. In our workshops, I show these figures and invite the participants to reflect on the fact that no one has yet written the book titled *Trust is Dead*, or *Trust Doesn't Work*, or *Trust is Yesterday's News*. No one has written those books because there is no evidence anywhere, whether it be from a leadership guru or an academic researcher, to support that point of view. This fact makes it even more surprising when we then realize that we have routinely been destroying trust in our institutional lives over the past 20 years.

Survey question 2 – perceptions of organizational trust

The data in Figure 7.4 comes from an established measure of organizational trust.[10] The eight statements reflect the three pillars of trust – ability, integrity and benevolence. The three trust pillars score a similar average, but the benevolence pillar is slightly weaker, which is consistent with popular perceptions of business life. From this data, we can see that organizations have the most scope to improve regarding their ability 'to do things competently' and their benevolence 'to go out of their way to help their stakeholders'. I encourage business leaders to think of the benevolence pillar as having been outsourced from business life as part of the agency theory model which did not need it. If you brought benevolence to your work in the industrial age then it was a nice-to-have by-product of being a human being rather than a must-have ingredient of business success. However, in the social age, if we want to build our cultures on trust, rather than power, it is time to insource benevolence because it has equal importance in the trust formula. Trustworthiness = ability × integrity x benevolence.

By averaging all the scores for the eight behaviours of organizational trust we can establish a benchmark organizational trust index of 5.6 out of 7. This trust index can then be tracked over time and compared with other organizations, so creating a genuine KPI for trust.

FIGURE 7.4   How trustworthy is your organization?

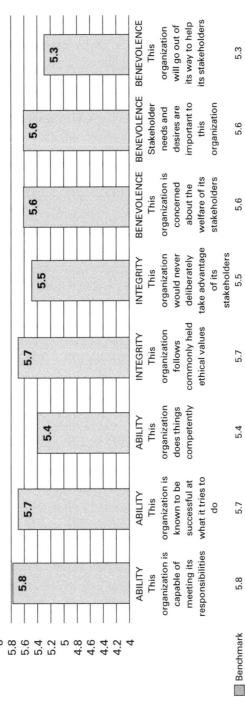

Average Score (Out of 7)

	ABILITY This organization is capable of meeting its responsibilities	ABILITY This organization is known to be successful at what it tries to do	ABILITY This organization does things competently	INTEGRITY This organization follows commonly held ethical values	INTEGRITY This organization would never deliberately take advantage of its stakeholders	BENEVOLENCE This organization is concerned about the welfare of its stakeholders	BENEVOLENCE Stakeholder needs and desires are important to this organization	BENEVOLENCE This organization will go out of its way to help its stakeholders
Benchmark	5.8	5.7	5.4	5.7	5.5	5.6	5.6	5.3

 Benchmark

Survey question 3 – perceptions of leadership trust

Figure 7.5 shows the ranking of the Nine Habits in the benchmark sample. The Honesty habit scores the highest by a significant margin, which is an encouraging finding given press headlines and scandals which often highlight lapses in business ethics and honesty. Our leaders regard our workplaces as honest environments. This is something we should not take for granted. Other strong habits are Deliver and Evangelize. The strength of the Delivery habit is not surprising, but it is interesting to note that our business leaders are influential evangelists, though this is a habit that can vary significantly across country cultures. I once delivered a workshop in Scotland, where the Evangelize habit was the most popular habit that leaders wanted to improve. 'We don't do evangelism in this country' explained one participant, alluding to the dour reputation of our Scottish compatriots.

The three weakest habits in the benchmark data are Be Open, Be Humble and Coach. In this sample, leaders still find it difficult to show vulnerability and share personal feelings in the workplace. They are not used to thinking of being humble as a strength and they are still telling their staff what to do, rather than coaching them through listening, asking and empowering. The benchmark results confirm some of the more anecdotal feedback from our clients:

'That word, vulnerability, was the challenge for all of us. It was my job to change people's perceptions of it, from seeing it as something very negative to help us all see what a powerful tool it can be' – Operations Manager, property sector

'Openness is the most critical habit for our organization. It's the openness of just straight talking that we've struggled with most' – CEO, charity sector

'Well, I think coaching is most critical to our success. The idea that you don't have to know all the answers and that by asking people questions, exciting their imaginations and drawing out their creativity, you boost performance. Ironically, this approach is very congruent with our business, which is all about creativity' – HR Director, entertainment sector

'We're going through a period of change over the next five years introducing technology into the workplace. So, we need more people who are ready to coach rather than shout. We want to focus more on becoming a coaching organization' – CEO, food retail sector

FIGURE 7.5 How trustworthy is your immediate manager?

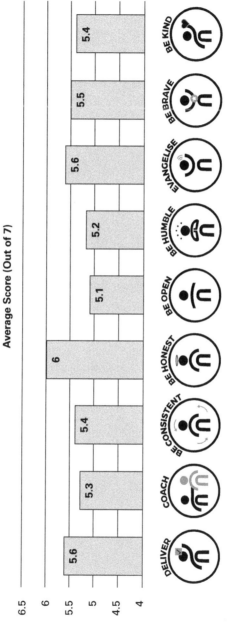

Average Score (Out of 7)

'Being Humble is critical to our success. We've got 5,000 employees and 3,500 of them are warehouse staff so it's really important for the leadership team to just be normal with everybody and not use distant managerial speak' – CEO, distribution sector

Similar to the organizational trust scores, we can average the Nine Habits scores to produce a leadership trust index of 5.5 out of 7. Note that there is a small difference between the benchmark organizational trust index of 5.6 and the leadership index of 5.5. As mentioned earlier, I refer to this difference as the 'authenticity gap'. In other words, if the organization is perceived as more trustworthy than its leaders then there is a risk that, over time, the internal leadership behaviour will undermine the perceptions of organizational trust.

Nine Habits leadership survey – behaviour rankings

Table 7.2 ranks all 27 behaviours in the Nine Habits measurement tool, from the strongest to the weakest, as averaged across all our survey responses.

TABLE 7.2   Ranking of Nine Habits behaviours

Habit and Behaviour	Mean Score
Honest – My line manager expects people to be scrupulously honest at work	6
Honest – My line manager demonstrates high standards of personal honesty	6
Honest – My line manager encourages honest and truthful workplace discussions	5.9
Deliver – My line manager is careful when making promises regarding commitments and deadlines	5.7
Evangelize – At work, it is clear to others that my line manager loves what he or she does	5.7
Brave – My line manager has the courage to act against the status quo when necessary	5.7

TABLE 7.2   *continued*

Habit and Behaviour	Mean Score
Humble – When things go well my line manager lets others take the praise	5.7
Kind – My line manager expects others to show care and kindness at work	5.6
Evangelize – My line manager is resilient to bounce back quickly from disappointments	5.6
Deliver – My line manager goes above and beyond what is expected in their key stakeholder relationships	5.6
Consistent – My line manager role-models our organizational values on a consistent basis	5.6
Consistent – My line manager makes decisions based on a clear set of personal values	5.6
Consistent – My line manager acts consistently despite changing circumstances	5.5
Kind – My line manager shows empathy and care when dealing with others at work	5.5
Evangelize – At work, my line manager promotes a passionate and inspiring vision	5.5
Open – My line manager is open to share personal thoughts and feelings at work	5.5
Brave – My line manager is brave enough to speak up for the wider good even at the expense of their own self-interest	5.5
Deliver – My line manager monitors and tracks the delegation and execution of tasks	5.4
Coach – My line manager is curious and asks questions of everyone in the team	5.4
Humble – When things go badly my line manager takes personal responsibility	5.4
Brave – My line manager praises others in the workplace who are brave to challenge the status quo	5.4
Coach – My line manager believes in people in the team and helps them achieve their full potential	5.3

TABLE 7.2   *continued*

Habit and Behaviour	Mean Score
Coach – My line manager listens to people in the team more than he or she talks to them	5.1
Open – My line manager is open with others about personal mistakes and failings	5
Open – My line manager praises people who show openness and vulnerability at work	5
Kind – My line manager practises random acts of kindness in the workplace	4.9
Humble – People would describe my line manager as a very humble person	4.6

Of most note in the rankings is the appearance of the Be Kind behaviour 'My line manager practises random acts of kindness in the workplace' in the bottom two. I regard this behaviour as the most significant 'quick win' opportunity for most leaders. It is a 'quick win' because random acts of kindness do not take a lot of time to deliver; they just take a lot of thought. Most leaders are very busy, but a 30-second random act of kindness can transform the workplace culture. A good example came from an HR Director in the way that he followed up our Trusted Executive workshop with his high-potential leaders. Each participant had left with one habit and one action to complete. The HR Director commented, 'I always make a note of what comes up for each of the participants and I send them a card with their particular habit as a Post-it note inside the card. And I guess that's a good example of how I'm trying to also role-model the habits. I hope it interprets as an act of kindness.' We can see from this example that even holding people accountable can be done in a kind way! Random acts of kindness are a power tool of leadership that most managers have never plugged in and learnt how to operate. The good news is that it is never too late in your career to start a new habit!

In this section, we have recognized the importance of goals, reporting and measurement in building a high-trust culture. Business is a performance sport. In any game, we need to know when we've crossed the finishing line. When we express our goals using the triple bottom line language of results, relationships and reputation, we ensure that the 'north star' of our business is tangible and measurable. If we then wish trust to be the glue that holds our cultures together, we need to find a way to measure trust as a leading indicator of success. The Nine Habits model provides that KPI because it is the first scientifically verified, behavioural measurement tool that allows a business to measure and benchmark trust, both at the brand and leadership levels. In the next section, we address a further challenge that all business leaders will face in the coming years – how to future-proof their businesses while under the scrutiny of investors increasingly focused on environmental, societal and governance (ESG) risks.

Using the Nine Habits to drive ESG (environmental, societal and governance) compliance

The term 'ESG investing' refers to the growing trend for investment analysts to evaluate environmental, societal and governance factors when assessing a company's future performance potential and strategic risk. The term was first coined in the landmark research article 'Who Cares Wins' in 2005.[11] These ESG factors include issues such as the corporate response to climate change, waste management, ethical supply chain management, social justice, employee representation, remuneration practices and board diversity. All these factors have not traditionally been part of financial analysis in the shareholder-dominated agency theory model of business. However, they are increasingly financially relevant in the stakeholder-dominated stewardship model.

Unlike its predecessor ethical investing, ESG investing is not a trade-off between financial performance and sound ethical practice. ESG investing relies on the increasing evidence that companies which score highly on ESG factors deliver superior financial returns and have a lower risk profile in a 'red pill' world where consumers and employees are voting with their feet concerning values-based decision making. In 2018, over $12 trillion of all assets under management were subject to ESG investment criteria. There are now hundreds of 'ESG analysts' working for the major institutional investment houses around the world.[12]

In his excellent *Forbes* article 'The Remarkable Rise of ESG',[13] Georg Kell summarizes this trend as follows:

> The big challenge for most corporations is to adapt to a new environment that
> favours smarter, cleaner and healthier products and services, and to leave behind

the dogmas of the industrial era when pollution was free, labour was just a cost factor and scale and scope was the dominant strategy.

In a nutshell, we are experiencing a shift from an industrial age where local consumers expected great products and services to a social age where global citizens expect not only great products and services, but also great companies – companies that contribute to society beyond the single bottom line of profit.

Recognizing this trend towards ESG investing and wishing to explore the links with building a high-trust culture, Edelman has extended its global trust barometer research to include tracking the views of institutional investors. In 2019, they surveyed 610 institutional investors across the countries of UK, US, Canada, Germany, Japan and the Netherlands who were managing assets totalling over $300 billion.[14] The research headlines are summarized below:

- 84 per cent of investors agreed that maximizing shareholder returns can no longer be the primary goal of business and that business leaders should commit to balancing the needs of shareholders with customers, employees, suppliers and local communities.

- Over 70 per cent believed having a high-trust reputation is important for attracting and retaining the best employees, winning new customers, growing market share and increasing market valuation.

- Over 50 per cent believed that ESG practices such as a healthy company culture, a diverse executive team and addressing societal issues positively impact trust

As can be seen, institutional investors expect a strong correlation between companies who are trusted and companies which score highly on ESG factors. Leaders who anticipate this trend will work out that one of the most compelling ways to convince investors of their ESG credentials will be to measure and showcase the trustworthiness of both their brand and their leaders. Such organizations will steal a competitive advantage. Our client, NAHL Group plc, instinctively grasped this connection and is now featuring the Nine Habits model as part of its annual report to communicate the steps they are taking to put trust at the heart of their organizational culture.[15] However, many other organizations are struggling to do this. According to a KPMG report, less than a quarter of businesses have successfully integrated ESG factors into their core business processes.[16] For leaders who wish to use the model for this purpose, the next section explores how each of the environmental, societal and governance factors map onto the Nine Habits.

Environmental factors

The most significant environmental issue under the scrutiny of investors is the corporate response to climate change; this is because climate change is not a distant, possible threat but an immediate, real phenomenon with multi-billion-dollar consequences. For several years, I have coached the CEO of a charity focused upon challenging corporate organizations to disclose their carbon footprints and to commit to the de-carbonization of their operations (CDP). Through this work, it has been fascinating to see how more and more organizations are declaring their carbon footprints and setting challenging targets for the future. For example, Microsoft's global operations have been 100 per cent net carbon neutral since 2012. The company charges a 'carbon fee' to all business groups for their carbon foot-print and invests the fees collected in its carbon reduction initiatives. Intel believes that employee engagement is essential to reaching the company's environmental goals, and since 2008 has tied a portion of each employee's compensation to corporate sustainability metrics. Finally, Accenture announced that it would aim to reduce its greenhouse gas emissions 11 per cent by 2025 – the largest professional services company to make this type of commitment.

Greta Thunberg has become the Gen Z spokesperson for the climate change movement and, in our Trusted Executive Foundation workshops, we challenge leaders to think about the question – 'Who is your Greta?' Who is the employee who is challenging the culture to face up to the climate change risk? If your company does not have a Greta then you should be looking to recruit one, rather than avoid the issue. Your Greta is coming, whether you plan for it or not, and it is always better to be a step ahead of the game. Managers manage. Leaders anticipate. Your Greta will help you identify the strategic risk to your brand and your leadership from the shifting expectations of the younger generations. As one of our client's HR directors put it, 'You know, as a father of teenagers, I know that they're different. And when they enter the workforce, they're not just interested in businesses that want to make money. They're interested in sustainability; they're interested in what those businesses are giving back to the world.'

Climate change is not the only environmental factor to focus upon. There are others, such as waste management and animal welfare. One of our clients, Suez UK, is in the waste management, recycling and energy recovery business and has over 5,500 employees. For the trust research, I interviewed former Suez UK CEO, David Palmer-Jones. It was fascinating to hear him talking about how public perceptions of the waste management sector have changed in recent years:

> Public exposure to our business has intensified over recent years as lots more waste and recycling facilities have come closer to people. With that came renewed media scrutiny of our operations, and greater awareness of the need to look after our environment. David Attenborough, in particular, doing a wonderful job of that.

As it happens, surveys have shown that Sir David Attenborough is one of the most trusted celebrities in the UK.[17] Through the power of his personal brand, he has transformed our collective attitude towards the management of plastic waste. For businesses like Suez UK, David Attenborough, like Greta Thunberg, is a strategic phenomenon. Such high-profile activists will become increasingly common in the years to come. Are you ready for your Greta or your David?

In thinking of which of the Nine Habits are most relevant to the environmental challenge of ESG, I would highlight Habits No.1 and No.7 – Deliver and Evangelize. First, there needs to be a triple bottom line vision with a planet-saving goal associated with climate change, waste management or similar 'change the world' agendas. Similar to Unilever's sustainable living plan and its ambition to halve Unilever's carbon footprint, every organization and CEO will need to evangelize its commitment in this area. Second, once the vision is declared, leaders must deliver on their ambition. Stakeholders are becoming ruthless in holding organizations accountable when it comes to 'walking the talk'. The phrases 'green-washing' and 'woke-washing' have become widespread to describe brands where the commitment to ESG actions is a superficial veneer, rather than a fully integrated part of their core processes and behaviours.

Societal factors

Whilst climate change is the headline issue involved in the environmental aspects of ESG, the societal factors are more varied and contextual.

Depending upon the sector and the country, issues such as diversity and inclusion, mental health, artificial intelligence, data privacy, social justice, ethical supply chains and modern slavery are all on the radar of corporate organizations. Each has the potential to either positively differentiate a brand or to turn a brand toxic.

The Trusted Executive Foundation is a preferred supplier of executive coaching to Jaguar Land Rover (JLR), one of the world's largest automotive manufacturers. Like many corporates, JLR is slowly but surely transforming from an aggressive, male-dominated, economically focused culture into something very different. As an example, the JLR approach to diversity and inclusion gives a proud voice to the LGBT community within the organization. Under the sponsorship of a board director, the LGBT community is being given a role in employee communications, alongside other minority groups, in a way that would have been unheard of just a few years ago. Similarly, the Trusted Executive Foundation partners with another bastion of traditional UK business, the Institute of Directors (IoD). We work with the IoD to support their diversity and inclusion seminars. Groundbreaking discussions have taken place in these seminars under the sponsorship of the IoD brand. Again, I could not have imagined these discussions happening even two or three years ago. It has highlighted to me how fast the social landscape of business is shifting.

At a more personal level, one of our trustees of the Trusted Executive Charitable Foundation, Steve Larke, is a partner at Deloitte and a champion of the mental health agenda in that business. Steve regularly shares his past struggles with his mental health both inside and outside the firm. Having known Steve for over 20 years, it has been inspiring to see how he has worked on the habits of being open and being brave to share his own story publicly. It is another example of how employees and customers are insisting on bringing their whole selves to the workplace, re-humanizing the world of business along the way. It is these habits of being open and being brave that will continue to catalyse the transforming of societal factors within high-trust organizations. We will increasingly find ourselves discussing topics in the boardroom that have not previously been on the business agenda. We will continue to witness brave leaders and brave brands challenging the status quo of business life. High-trust cultures will hold the necessary conversations in psychologically safe environments, allowing them to adapt to new social realities, rather than risk being left behind. Building a high-trust culture prepares your business for these coming changes.

Governance factors

The governance aspects of ESG include topics such as board diversity, executive remuneration and ownership structure. For example, how much difference does it make if you are a leader committed to building a high-trust culture in a public limited company (plc), an owner-managed firm, a charity or a private equity-owned business? The widespread assumption is that it is harder to build trust in companies led by owners focused only on driving short-term financial results. This style of governance is the traditional agency theory creation that we discussed in Chapter 1. Surprisingly, the views of CEOs I interviewed varied on this issue. Some strongly endorsed the layman's view:

> The investment criterion for a private equity firm is not, 'Is this an ethical and honest business?' It's not even on the radar. They might find a few CSR boxes to tick at the end of the year, but it is not why they are going to invest.

Others challenged this perception:

> In theory, a partnership structure should be more conducive to building trustworthiness through shared ownership. In practice, I don't think it makes one iota of difference. I really don't. This is because you have got egocentric, domineering, 'I know best' leaders in all types of organizations – public sector, private sector, SMEs, not-for-profits.

Likewise, in my career, I have had mixed experiences in different ownership environments that have convinced me that trustworthiness can be built or destroyed in any governance structure depending upon the leadership personalities involved. That said, we can expect a growing shift towards more employee ownership and board representation in future governance models to mitigate the risk that employee activism will undermine a brand's reputation. Alongside increased employee representation, other aspects of board roles and diversity will continue to come under scrutiny. There has been a drive on UK boards to separate the roles of the Chairman and CEO and increase the number of female board members. Other countries are taking similar steps. Less high-profile, but critical to building a high-trust culture, is the ongoing debate about the need for one board member to have a dedicated focus on the company's ESG responsibilities. For example, as Unilever pursued its triple bottom line vision, a new role was created called Chief Marketing, Communications and Sustainability Officer – a bit of a mouthful but an influential role sitting on the main board and reporting directly to the CEO. The CEOs I interviewed highlighted similar expectations for future board governance:

> 'One of the things that is going to change is the development of the "customer director" role who owns the holistic customer experience end-to-end across all channels to market. These customer directors will be the CEOs of the future.'

> 'Brands could be the driver of trustworthiness, but that would need the Chief Marketing Officer to sit on the board or become the CEO.'

If there is one structural change that is demanded by the red pill world, it is that the ESG voice must be heard more directly in the boardroom. This voice must be at least equal in authority and empowerment to the view of the CFO.

Last but not least, we come to the sensitive topic of remuneration and incentives. Let's imagine that you are the CEO of a global multinational, your business is pursuing the triple bottom line of results, relationships and reputation, you have personally mastered the Nine Habits and your organization has integrated all ESG factors into your core business roles and processes. Yet, you still earn an annual salary of $1.6 million and you have share options worth a further $2 million and a pension pot of $17 million. Are your stakeholders going to trust you? Or will they think that you live in a different world? A world where, from their perspective, the odds are stacked in your favour. Because the bottom line is that, as one of the CEOs I interviewed put it, 'What undermines trust is when people perceive the risk/reward ratio is not fair across society.' Here is a longer excerpt from a private company CEO that highlights the strength of feeling on this topic from inside the boardroom itself:

> Let's face it, it's not good if you put your money on the counter and you can't trust you're going to get the right interest rate, whilst the chief executive of the bank is giving himself a €10 million bonus. How does that work? Why would you be earning a thousand times more than your employees?

If this is how seasoned CEOs regard the situation, then what of other stakeholders who have never stepped foot inside a corporate business? In the UK, we have already seen the introduction of gender pay gap reporting and the disclosure of pay ratios, ie the difference between the pay of the highest-paid and lowest-paid people in the organization. Shareholder groups continue to lobby to curb excessive pay and bonuses in plc boardrooms. While it may be the last sacred blue pill cow to be slaughtered, it is hard to see how high-trust organizations will be able to 'walk the talk' without facing up to this perceived lack of fairness inherent to corporate remuneration practices.

Tackling these governance challenges of ESG will require two habits in particular from the Nine Habits model – choosing to be humble and choosing to be consistent. Humble CEOs and CFOs will let go of the power and entitlement of the blue pill, agency theory boardroom to welcome the voice of those who have traditionally had less power – women, employees, CMOs, etc. As they do this, they will also demonstrate the humility to bring more consistency and fairness into the workplace, particularly in how the financial rewards of success are shared amongst a broad stakeholder base. Investors will increasingly reward these behaviours as they see the positive impacts on both financial performance and brand reputation.

Interview with Russell Atkinson, CEO, NAHL Group plc

In concluding this chapter, and indeed this book, I would like to give the final words to the winner of our first 'Trusted Executive of the Year' award, Russell Atkinson, CEO of NAHL Group plc. NAHL Group plc is the parent company of National Accident Helpline (NAH), Fitzalan Partners, Searches UK and Bush & Company Rehabilitation. NAHL Group was established in 1993 and has grown to an industry-leading position as an outsourced marketing services provider, assisting genuine accident victims in seeking compensation and redress for injuries. I first met Russell in 2017 when I delivered a 'Trusted Executive' workshop to his Vistage CEO group. Russell was one of those leaders who immediately 'got it'. He was already a believer in the power of trust. As he later put it in the company's annual report:

> When I was introduced to the Trusted Executive Framework, I knew I'd
> found something that chimed with the very essence of our business. I had been
> searching for a framework compatible with the personality, values, and ethos of
> NAHL. So it was something of a 'Eureka!' moment when I was introduced to
> Dr John Blakey and his Trusted Executive leadership model.[17]

Russell and his leadership team took to the Nine Habits like ducks to water. They rolled out the framework and put it at the heart of their recruitment, their appraisal systems and their leadership development. In so doing, they started to use the model in ways that I had not previously envisaged, including inviting members of their teams to blog on each habit and present to each other on ideas and best practice in implementing the model. It was quite a shock the day that one of Russell's leadership team sent me a photo showing a four-foot-high Nine Habits diagram painted on their office wall in Kettering. At first, I thought it was some photoshop special effect, but later I realized they had similar Nine Habits diagrams posted all around the business. They were taking it seriously! As a result of their focus on building a high-trust culture, NAH is the most trusted brand in the UK personal injury market and it has the top click-through rate to its website. It was recognized by the *Sunday Times* as one of the top 100 best small companies to work for in 2019 and received an Investors in People Gold status award to go alongside their Silver award in Critical Care. It has also seen significant improvements in employee engagement scores across the Group – well ahead of national averages. Early in 2019, I interviewed Russell for the Trusted Executive Foundation blog post series to capture his experience working with the Nine Habits model.[18] Here are some excerpts from that interview to close out this chapter hearing from someone who has excelled at 'walking the talk' of trust:

John: How have you worked with the Trusted Executive Foundation?

Russell: We've completed two 'Trusted Executive' workshops with our leadership teams and we did another session at our annual management conference where everybody worked in small groups and talked about which of the Nine Habits they'd been working on. Where I am lucky is that because we have recruited in line with our values, it has been really easy to get senior management buy-in. I haven't been pushing against a closed door. Marcus, our HR Director, loves it all. Even our CFO, James, loves it. He gets involved and understands its value! We've all got a picture of the model on our desks and walls. From time to time, we will remind ourselves of why we are working in this way. If I see behaviours that are working against the Nine Habits or our values, then I will call those out. When we do our coaching and we do our appraisals, we do ask, 'How are you doing on our values and on the Nine Habits?'

John: Which habits did you already have as strengths in the NAHL Group culture?

Russell: I think there were two habits that were already well-embedded. Habit No.5 – being open with people – and Habit No.6 – being humble and knowing that 'this isn't all about me'. My own leadership is a coaching style (Habit No.2) because I know I'm not the best strategist in the world, or the best marketing person in the world, or the best salesperson in the world. But I like to think I'm reasonable at most things and therefore can have a view and I try to coach people to do that. So I use coaching, linked to openness and humility, as a natural style that I have and then I build upon that. I think you have to walk the walk. There is no point talking all day about being trusted but if you're not open with people, if you're not honest with people, if you hide things, then you're in a bit of trouble trying to get that message across.

I just see myself as a bloke from Newcastle who got lucky. You get into the CEO role and you're thinking, 'I'm not quite sure how I got here but hey-ho I'll do it my way and I'll do my little bit.' I don't always get it right I'm sure, but there are certain rules I try and follow. I do recognize that my demeanour within the organization, whatever I'm thinking of, whatever pressures I have, sets the tone. If you set a cheerful and reasonably positive tone, then that's a positive. I never shout at people, but I know some CEOs that do that or are unpredictable and it's the unpredictability that's the hard part. If they're in a great mood and you think, 'Oh this is brilliant, the best person I've ever worked for', and then the next day they're bawling you out for one reason or another, that's dreadful. You've got to be consistent (Habit No.3).

John: Which habits are you now focusing on and why?

Russell: We're moving our business model from a cash upfront claims aggregator into a law firm. It's like a Formula One car driving around a track – you're changing the wheels and the tyres and turning it into a rally car – but still driving it. So I would say one habit we're focusing upon is being brave (Habit No.8). I'm trying to make sure that we don't get too bold. The danger of having a strength like bravery is that you might think, 'Well, we've been impregnable, we've become untouchable and then let's be bold about that and let's be bold about this.' I have to make sure that our team are looking very carefully at things that they're taking a proper analytical view, assessing the risks, then being bold. Don't just be bold because you feel brave. Be bold because you have the right tools to do it.

Another habit we are focusing upon is the habit of evangelizing (Habit no.7) and it's something that we do well internally, but we don't do it externally. There's a tension with the other habit of being humble (Habit

No.6). We're not very good at banging our own drum and it can cost us a little bit if we're not out there saying, 'Actually this has gone really well, we've made some good decisions here.' That works against me a little bit because it's not my natural style to say, 'Look how good we are', but somehow you have to do it.

Finally, the kindness habit is interesting (Habit No.9) and the idea of practising random acts of kindness. Last year we gave all our employees an extra day's holiday to reward their efforts. That was a gesture, but I don't think it was a random act of kindness because it was planned and it was motivational, so I don't count that. However, if I make somebody a cup of tea (the word CEO does not mean I can't make tea!), then I do think that's a random act of kindness. It's the little things, not the big things. I have a colleague who is a naturally kind person. Somebody came to her who was really struggling at home and she phoned me up immediately to ask if we could give them a loan. That wasn't my random act of kindness, that was her saying, how do I help this individual? And that's true kindness.

John: You've had a 360 feedback using the Nine Habits model. What did you get out of that experience?

Russell: I think it was very interesting to see how the results compared and how people saw me against the Nine Habits and where people saw my team. The 360 reports helped me take a look at my team and say, where do we need to do a bit more work? It sets the baseline for us to build from and it helps me understand the dynamic of my team. The biggest challenge we've got is to retain the levels of trust that we've already reached and make sure we keep an eye on all of the different habits because although one habit doesn't make the model, getting it really badly wrong on one habit can break the model.

John: Finally, why do you think it is important for a company like yours to focus upon trust in these current times?

Russell: The world is going through a period of change more profound than anything we've seen since the Industrial Revolution. As well as the widespread presence of technology and constant regulatory change, one of the biggest changes we are seeing is that of personal attitudes. Power, once the epicentre of decision making for business leaders and customers, has been replaced with trust and a desire to see the 'right thing' being done. We've all seen how trust has been lost in established institutions, from finance and politics, through to the charity sector – with ethics called into question and reputations left in tatters. And what's more, no organization is immune; only recently Google had to respond to an empowered workforce demanding trust and transparency from their leaders.

We have transitioned into a world where business success is now about dealing with change and uncertainty at high speed, and doing it ethically. Equipping ourselves to deal with these changes is crucial to our continued success as an organization. It means being open to change and evolution while, at the same time, retaining our core values. As this journey progresses, we will go on to identify elements and further support our people with their personal development, nurturing skills – helping them and equipping them for a changing workplace and a changing world.

POINTS TO PONDER

- Share the results of your Nine Habits self-assessment from the earlier chapters with your team member, manager and peers. What new insights can they provide to ensure you eliminate any blind spots and capitalize on any hidden strengths?

- Think of your current team. What stage of the Tuckman model do you think you are in? How are you responding to the challenges of that stage and how might the Nine Habits model help you?

- Which of the Nine Habits would emerge from a survey of your leaders as most critical for your organization?

- What would be the triple bottom line goals and associated KPIs for your organization covering results, relationships and reputation?

- If Greta Thunberg or David Attenborough visited your organization for a week, what issues do you think she or he would raise with your board?

- How could you review your top team to ensure the voice of ESG is heard as loudly as the voice of the CFO?

- Work in small groups of two or three with your peers and discuss the role of executive remuneration in building high-trust cultures.

Endnotes

1 Blakey, J S (2019) *CEO/Senior Leader Trustworthy Behaviours and their Role in Promoting Organisational Trustworthiness*, Aston Business School

2 The Trusted Executive Foundation (2017) Donald Trump and the Nine Habits of Trust, https://trustedexecutive.com/donald-trump-nine-habits-trust/ (archived at https://perma.cc/AU74-EQGX)

3 Goman, C K (2013) *The Truth about Lies in the Workplace: How to spot liars and what to do about them*, Berrett-Koehler Publishers

4 Brett, J and Mitchell, T (2020) How to build trust with business partners form other cultures, *Harvard Business Review*, https://hbr.org/2020/01/research-how-to-build-trust-with-business-partners-from-other-cultures (archived at https://perma.cc/59ZV-4NJ6)

5 Duhigg, C (2016) What Google learned from its quest to build the perfect team, *New York Times Magazine*, 28 February

6 Lencioni, P (2006) *The Five Dysfunctions of a Team*, John Wiley & Sons

7 Bonebright, D A (2010) 40 years of storming: a historical review of Tuckman's model of small group development, *Human Resource Development International*, **13** (1), pp 111–20

8 Covey, S R (1994) *Seven Habits of Highly Effective People*, Simon and Schuster

9 Populus (2011) The trust deficit: views from the boardroom, https://www.dlapiper.com/en/dubai/insights/publications/2011/10/the-trust-deficit-views-from-the-boardroom/ (archived at https://perma.cc/AFA7-3GEK)

10 Searle, R, Weibel, A and Den Hartog, D N (2011) Employee trust in organizational contexts, *International Review of Industrial and Organizational Psychology*, **26**

11 UN Global Compact (2004) Who Cares Wins, https://d306pr3pise04h.cloudfront.net/docs/issues_doc%2FFinancial_markets%2Fwho_cares_who_wins.pdf (archived at https://perma.cc/XHJ2-A6Q7)

12 US/SIF Foundation (2018) Report on US Sustainable, Responsible and Impact Investing Trends 2018, https://www.ussif.org/files/Trends/Trends%202018%20executive%20summary%20FINAL.pdf (archived at https://perma.cc/JUG6-BJLH)

13 Kell, G (2018) The Remarkable Rise of ESG, *Forbes*, https://www.forbes.com/sites/georgkell/2018/07/11/the-remarkable-rise-of-esg/ (archived at https://perma.cc/6BG4-W75C)

14 Edelman (2019) 2019 Edelman Trust Barometer – Special Report – Institutional Investors – Global Report, https://www.edelman.com/sites/g/files/aatuss191/files/2019-12/2019%20Edelman%20Trust%20Barometer%20Special%20Report%20-%20Investor%20Trust.pdf (archived at https://perma.cc/UDN9-55JH)

15 NAHL Group plc (2019) Annual Report and Accounts 2018 p 23, https://www.nahlgroupplc.co.uk/storage/app/media/annual-report-2018-web-version.pdf (archived at https://perma.cc/N4U4-VHPY)

16 KPMG (2018) ESG, Risk, and Return – A Board's Eye View, https://assets.kpmg/content/dam/kpmg/be/pdf/2018/05/esg-risk-and-return.pdf (archived at https://perma.cc/TNR6-GV5U)

17 UNILAD (2018) Sir David Attenborough is Britain's most trusted celebrity, https://www.unilad.co.uk/life/sir-david-attenborough-is-britains-most-trusted-celebrity/ (archived at https://perma.cc/96LW-S24B)

18 The Trusted Executive Foundation (2019) The Nine Habits of Trust in Action: walking the talk with Russell Atkinson – CEO, NAHL Group plc, https://trustedexecutive.com/the-nine-habits-in-action-walking-the-talk-with-russell-atkinson-ceo-nahl-group-plc/ (archived at https://perma.cc/6DT5-YL5E)

Conclusion

'Well done, Blakey'

Time to make a choice

'I know what you're thinking, 'cause right now I'm thinking the same thing. Actually, I've been thinking it ever since I got here, Why, oh why, didn't I take the blue pill?' Cypher to Neo (*The Matrix*)

Since I left my corporate career at the age of 39, I have often thought of Cypher's lament from the film *The Matrix*. I was international managing director in a FTSE 100 company. I had grown my business from annual revenues of £200 million to £370 million. According to many, I was on an 'interesting career path'. One colleague put words to other people's concerns when he said, 'John, I don't understand it. It seems to me you're giving up an exciting career in leadership to become... a coach?' The words hung in the air. I didn't have an immediate answer to his accusation that I was prematurely hanging up my leadership boots.

In the months following that choice, there were many fretful nights. As a novice executive coach, I didn't feel important. I had no formal authority, no impressive job title, no armies of staff around the world and, at times, I struggled to understand how executive coaching could really be the next stage of an interesting career in leadership. Most of my career, I had walked into rooms wanting to be the most powerful person in the room. Often, I *was* the most powerful person in the room. It was everything I knew. It was everything for which I had been groomed. Now I was walking into rooms as the least powerful person in the room. It forced me to build a new leadership currency based on trust because there was no other choice. It was only in those moments that I realized how difficult it is to walk the talk of the Nine Habits and become the most trusted one. I had a lot to learn.

At times, I rebelled against the trust curriculum. I wanted to go back to the world of power. I felt part of me yearning to be someone like Tim Armstrong – the all-powerful former leader of AOL. A man lauded as a genius by AOL's shareholders when he announced he was selling AOL to Verizon for $4.4 billion in May 2015. Yet also a man who was famously described by Lucy Kellaway of the *Financial Times* as 'one of the least appealing figures in corporate life'.[1] In the Verizon deal, Mr Armstrong netted a personal fortune of $180 million. In an interview with CNN, he credits his success to his father, a Vietnam veteran, who taught him, 'Do whatever it takes to be successful'. In his case, doing whatever it takes included publicly sacking one of his senior staff in front of 1,000 colleagues for taking a photo with his smartphone. 'You're fired – out!' he bellows in the infamous YouTube clip of the incident, before calmly proceeding with the all-staff conference call.[2] Oh, to be that ruthless. Oh, to be that thick-skinned.

However, today, I am proud of my 39-year-old self. Without his choice, I would not have found my true leadership purpose. I'm glad I took the red pill, but it has taken me 17 years to climb this new mountain – the mountain of trust. I am not at the top of that mountain, but there are times when I get some incredible views from being halfway up. The most moving moments have come from an exercise that I facilitate in the longer two-day Trusted Executive workshops. I typically start day two with an exercise I call 'The Trust Wall'. By this time, the participants are willing to be more open, so I ask them the question, 'Who in your life or work do you trust the most and why?' After a minute of reflection, I invite them to write the name of their most trusted person on a large whiteboard at the front of the room. One by one, they come up, select a whiteboard marker and contribute to building the trust wall. Here are some examples of what they write:

'My youngest son – he is always there to hear my story.'

'My brother – he saved my life.'

'My ex-boss – he gave me the freedom to make decisions.'

'My mother – she never lies, she never bullshits me.'

'My colleague – she is reliable and practical. She goes the extra mile.'

Once fully populated, the 'trust wall' becomes a sacred object. I invite everyone around the whiteboard to honour the most trusted ones. As I read out what people have written, I can see tears in people's eyes and smiles of pure joy on their faces. 'Aren't these people so special?' I declare. Everyone violently nods in agreement. It is a wonderful, celebratory occasion.

At the end of the exercise, I challenge the participants to imagine that I had invited their own teams into the room and asked them the same question. Would their names appear on the trust walls of their own team members? Is that a legacy of which they would be proud? Is that how they want to be remembered? As Trusted Executives? As the most trusted person in the room? It is in those moments that I am glad I took the red one and started to climb a new mountain because, in those moments, I realize that I didn't give up an interesting career in leadership, I simply started to think of leadership in a different way.

Today, I work with many different CEOs around the world who have made a similar choice to the one I made all those years ago. Leaders who are relying upon the power of trust rather than trusting in power, whether that be in enlightened global corporates or disruptive SMEs. I am greatly encouraged by the emergence of this breed of brave leaders who are putting their heads above the institutional parapets to challenge the prevailing way. It is no revolution, but I do sense an evolution and one that is gaining momentum. In their book *King, Warrior, Magician, Lover*,[3] Doug Gillette and Robert Moore (1991) talk of the challenge of making these pivotal transitions: 'Ours is a psychological age rather than an institutional one. What used to be done for us by institutional structures and through ritual process, we now have to do inside ourselves, for ourselves.' I think it is a similar challenge as executive leadership matures from its heroic to its post-heroic age; from agency theory to stewardship. We need to do this work on ourselves first by making new choices and climbing new mountains. For all of us, it is a work in process, but I can summarize the choice we all face through the following leadership invitation:

Untrustworthy agent was a role given to you by the industrial revolution and its 19th-century architects. Those architects were economists at heart. Trusted steward is a role offered to you by the social revolution and its 21st-century architects. Those new architects are psychologists at heart. The red pill of transparency will progressively reveal this reality to you and your peers. You will then be faced with a choice. By definition, the trusted steward role must be chosen by you, not imposed upon you by an institutional framework. Denial was previously the means of ducking that choice, yet that option is not available in a red pill world where transparency leaves no place to hide. Delusion is the only modern alternative. In its final throes, the agency theory paradigm will throw up a range of deluded leaders. You may be able to think of one or two that are appearing in the business and political system right now! Be careful not to mistake their headline-grabbing antics for a symptom of the enduring strength of the old world as opposed to the proximity of the new; untrustworthy agents make for good headlines; trusted stewards make for no headlines at all.

You will make your choice and others will make theirs. Not everyone will be a believer in the power of trust. Some people will call us dreamers… but we're not the only ones. As you come to the end of this book, it is time to make a choice. What is your choice going to be?

Seizing the prize (or not)

I hope this book has been thought-provoking, but more than that I hope this book has been a call to action. To borrow and transpose the Joker's twisted wisdom in the film *The Dark Knight*, 'Sanity is a lot like gravity; all it requires is a little push.' I hope this book represents that little push. I also hope that this book helps you understand how to 'do' trusted stewardship through the three pillars and nine leadership habits we have explored. First, the three habits of ability that ensure you and your team consistently deliver results that make an impact on the triple bottom line. Second, the three habits of integrity that will ensure you role-model honesty, openness and humility in your interactions with all the stakeholders of the modern business. Third, the three habits of benevolence that will ensure your evangelical passion, your moral bravery and your kindness will leave a legacy of which a future generation will be proud. Above all, remember author David Marquet's concise advice: 'Bosses think their way to new action. Leaders act their way to new thinking'.[4] Use the DO HB CHECK questionnaires, work the exercises, take the next step, make a mistake, start again; that is how the nine leadership habits will turn from the theory into the practice.

FIGURE 8.1   The Nine Habits of Trust

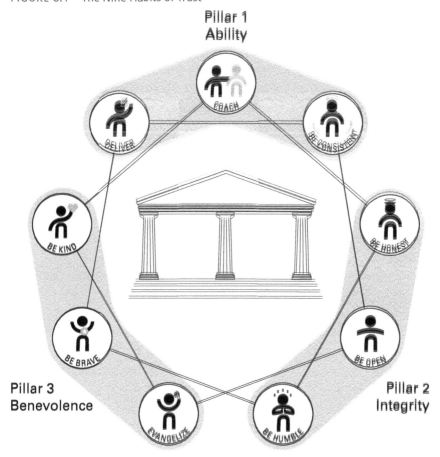

Pillar 1
Ability

Pillar 3
Benevolence

Pillar 2
Integrity

As you use the exercises, questionnaires and case studies in this book, remember that trust is an incredibly valuable commodity; it is like a fossil fuel. It takes years to create and it disappears in a flash. The trust in our institutions was created by the trusted stewards of a much earlier age. We have lived off their legacy for generations. The authority it gave to our leaders fuelled the industrial revolution. Yet we are now running out of those reserves. It is time for a new generation of trusted executives, like you, to create a fresh store of trust; not by digging ever deeper for renewed authority, but through returning to the original trust-building process and mastering its raw materials: ability, integrity and benevolence. Yes, this will take time, but, unlike the process for creating fossil fuels, this timescale does not have to be left to nature alone. We can accelerate the speed with which the reserves of trust are replenished by reinventing our perceptions of leadership. Under the guidance of trusted executives, our organizations can be transformed into powerhouses of triple bottom line productivity underpinned by high-trust relationships.

The prize for those who pursue this path will be significant. As one FTSE 100 director put it, 'If everyone else is losing trust, those of us who can hold onto it... will stand out ever more strongly from the rest'.[5] Trust is a strategic, competitive advantage both for the individual and the organization. Pursuing the triple bottom line of results, relationships and reputation is a leap of faith. It requires courage. In the moment that we reach for these higher goals, we might fear that we will sacrifice everything that went before. The trusted executives of tomorrow will feel this fear and will do it anyway. They will then experience that this is not a sacrificial model. Pursuing the triple bottom line does not mean sacrificing profit – it means going beyond profit.

The evidence suggests that companies that do good will also do well in the red pill world. In the United States, the organization Trust Across America has been tracking the performance of the most trustworthy public companies in the US since 2009. Those companies have produced an 81.6 per cent return on investment in that period versus the 46.3 per cent return of the 500 largest listed companies in the United States.[6] In a separate piece of research, Dr Fred Kiel collected data on 84 CEOs over a seven-year period and found that what he called 'high integrity' CEOs had a multi-year return of 9.4 per cent, compared to 'low-integrity' CEOs who generated a mere 1.9 per cent over the same period.[7]

As I write this conclusion, a quarter of the world's population is in lockdown due to the coronavirus pandemic. There is loss of life on a colossal scale. You, the reader, may know how this all pans out, but currently, I do not. Right now, there is much fear, anxiety and a real sense of grief. Some are grieving from personal loss, while others are grieving from a sense that our world will never be the same again. After months of virtual, socially distanced working, how will the world of work emerge from this crisis? How will we cope with what seems like an inevitable global recession? What new leadership challenges will need to be mastered in the 'new normal' that awaits us on the other side?

Yet, even as we watch daily TV screens showing the suffering and the pain, there is already talk that this crisis may represent a turning point. A turning point in how we manage our health and well-being. A turning point in how we connect and care for each other. A turning point in how we take care of the planet. A turning point in the nature of leadership. There is the potential for this to be a collective 'red pill' moment. The point at which we all make new choices together to create a world founded on trust, rather than one founded on power. Who knows? It will come down to the choices we all make as we journey through these unique times. I hope that we seize the prize and do not miss the opportunity of a lifetime.

The end of the beginning

At the beginning of this book I committed to walking the tightrope between logic, analysis, structure and imagination, passion, flair. I intended to write a book that bridges the academic and the pragmatic. In treading this tightrope, I have resisted the temptation to feature a poem. So far. However, I hope that, at this stage of the journey, we have built enough trust between us that you will indulge me with the following abridged verse from D H Lawrence's poem *Trust*:

> Oh we've got to trust
> one another again
> in some essentials.
>
> Not the narrow little
> bargaining trust
> that says: I'm for you
> if you'll be for me.
>
> But a bigger trust,
> a trust of the sun
> that does not bother
> about moth and rust,
>
> ...
> And be, oh be
> a sun to me,
> not a weary, insistent
> personality
>
> but a sun that shines
> and goes dark, but shines
> again and entwines
> with the sunshine in me

Whatever new business landscape emerges post-COVID-19, I urge you to be a sun to all the stakeholders in your business and to inspire them to trust again; not a narrow, bargaining trust, but a bigger trust of ability, integrity and benevolence. A trust that inspires others, so that they can then be a sun to you. A trust that creates a proud legacy for your organization. A trust that shines.

To close, I'd like to revisit the story from the Introduction when you will recall I was found guilty of being 'too f-ing nice' by a company managing director in my earlier career. The story did not end there. I walked away from that bruising exchange with a conviction to prove a point; a conviction to prove that nice folk, leaders who can be trusted, can also deliver outstanding bottom line results. Some years later, I found myself presenting on the performance of my business unit to the same managing director during a company board meeting. The day had been the usual gladiatorial contest in which many had been given the grim 'thumbs down' from our insatiable boss. There was blood on the walls and I feared I was the next lamb to the slaughter. But, nevertheless, I launched into my presentation with gusto, armed with a highly impressive set of key performance indicators. At the end of my stint, I could see others around the table bracing themselves for what they thought was coming next. But today was different. As I tided up my papers, the managing director leant forward across the table and said slowly, 'I don't often say this, Blakey, but... well done.' You could have heard a pin drop. In the distance, I am sure a choir of angels burst into a spontaneous 'Hallelujah' chorus. I replied with a stunned 'thanks' and quickly departed the room. My colleague, who had been stood at the door, rushed up behind me and asked, 'What happens now?' I thought for a moment, realized I'd come to the end of the story and said, 'I guess it's time to resign.' Managers manage. Leaders anticipate.

Thank you for staying the course. Keep taking the red one!

Endnotes

1 Kellaway, L (2015) A harsh lesson from the very unappealing boss of AOL, *Financial Times*, 19 May

2 Ibid

3 Gillette, D and Moore, R (1991) *King, Warrior, Magician, Lover*, HarperCollins, New York

4 Marquet, L D (2013) *Turn the Ship Around! A true story of turning followers into leaders*, Penguin, Harmondsworth

5 Populus (2011) *The Trust Deficit: Views from the boardroom*, Populus, London

6 Kimmel, B B (2015) Will 2015 be 'The Year of Trust' or just more of the same?

7 Kiel, F (2015) *Return on Character: The real reason leaders and their companies win*, Harvard Business Review Press, Boston, MA

AFTERWORD

If you have enjoyed reading this book, please submit an honest review to your local Amazon site.

If you wish to join an international community of trusted executives who are focused on mastering the Nine Habits, please get in touch with the team at the Trusted Executive Foundation via www.trustedexecutive.com.

If you want to become an accredited Trusted Executive coach with a licence to use the Nine Habits model in your part of the world, please contact us via info@trustedexecutive.com.

ABOUT THE AUTHOR

Dr John Blakey is the founder of the Trusted Executive Foundation, a not-for-profit organization that helps board-level teams build high-performance cultures underpinned by the values of trust and challenge. The mission of the Foundation is to create a new standard of leadership defined by trustworthiness and to gift over £1m to UK Christian-led charities over the next 10 years. The Trusted Executive Foundation delivers 'Journey of Trust' leadership development programmes based on the tools and models in John's acclaimed books, *The Trusted Executive* and *Challenging Coaching*. *Challenging Coaching*, co-authored with Ian Day, is one of the UK's best-selling leadership books and features the FACTS coaching model. It was inspired by Dr Blakey's executive coaching work helping over 130 CEOs from 22 different countries to achieve courageous goals, as well as the leaders of gold-medal-winning Team GB Olympic squads, premiership football clubs and England cricket. Dr Blakey delivers keynote speaker sessions at leadership conferences globally and supports a small number of pioneering, UK-based CEOs each year as an executive coach. His work has been featured in *Forbes, BBC News, HuffPost, Inc. Magazine*, the *FT* and the *Sunday Times*.

ACKNOWLEDGEMENTS

Thank you to my coaching clients over the past 17 years who have shown me the possibility and potential of the trusted steward role, role-modelled the Nine Habits and renewed my faith in executive leadership.

Thank you to all the CEOs who gave their valuable time to be interviewed and who generously offered their wisdom and experience.

Thank you to Professor John Rudd, Professor Ann Davis and Dr Alison LeGood for their expert supervision of my doctoral thesis, and all my colleagues on the DBA programme at Aston Business School.

Thank you to all the people who trusted me in my career, in particular, Graham Nye (British Gas), John Robson (British Gas), Iain Barker (Team 121), Dr Martin Read CBE (Logica), Bill Barry (121 partners), Nicholas Brealey (*Challenging Coaching*) and Steve Gilroy (Vistage).

Thank you to all the team and partners at the Trusted Executive Foundation for creating a vehicle through which the theory of the Nine Habits is now being put into practice around the world.

Thank you to all at Kogan Page for their professionalism and care in publishing this work.

Last but not least, thank you to my wife, Jane, for her love and support throughout my career.

Soli Deo gloria.

INDEX

CPSIA information can be obtained
at www.ICGtesting.com
Printed in the USA
LVHW070049040922
727549LV00047B/1139

9 781789 666458